MW01142891

THE CHRISTIAN HELL

FROM THE FIRST TO THE
TWENTIETH CENTURY

WATTS'S 9d. NET SERIES.

Each pocket size, bound in cloth.

---

*(N.B.—Postage on one book, 2d. or 3d.;
on two books, 3d. or 4d.; and so on.)*

SATAN, CASED IN ARMOUR, CRUNCHING SINNERS IN
THE GULF OF HELL.
(From Didron's *Christian Iconography*.)

THE

CHRISTIAN HELL

FROM THE FIRST TO THE
TWENTIETH CENTURY

BY

HYPATIA BRADLAUGH BONNER

[ISSUED FOR THE RATIONALIST PRESS ASSOCIATION, LIMITED]

With Twenty-Eight Illustrations

LONDON :
WATTS & CO.,
17 JOHNSON'S COURT, FLEET STREET, E.C.
1913

CONTENTS

LIST OF ILLUSTRATIONS

PREFACE

"WHAT old woman is so stupid now as to tremble at those tales of hell which were once so firmly believed in?" asked Cicero nearly two thousand years ago. This belief in an afterworld of pain, so scornfully rejected by the pagan philosophers, was made the cornerstone of the new Christian religion, and from the first century of the Christian era to the twentieth it has done more to poison the wells of human happiness than any other evil, real or imaginary, known to mankind.

Many books have been written upon the eschatology of the Christian religion, but the earlier ones were avowedly for the purpose of maintaining the reality of the last judgment and enlarging upon the awful fate which awaited the sinner in hell, while the object of most of the more recent is to deny that reality, and to explain away the terrors. The books which have dealt with this subject from a really critical and historical point of view are few and far between, and have the disadvantage that they are written from the theistic standpoint. In any case they are bulky volumes, more suited to the theological student or the man of leisure than for the information of the general public. Within the narrow limits of the following pages, I have endeavoured briefly to set forth the nature of the teaching of the Christian Churches in English-speaking countries, and, even at the risk of becoming wearisome, I have so far as possible given either the actual words or a brief *résumé* of the words of those whose authority has been accepted, or whose influence has been of weight in some or other of the various sects which are sheltered under the name of Christianity.

The subject is one which urgently calls for free and open discussion upon serious lines, and should no longer be confined to the jester or to the timid utterances of clerics, who are necessarily hampered by the consciousness that any but the most superficial criticism is bound to undermine the creed which they have made it the business of their lives to disseminate and uphold. A sane and sound morality has everything to gain from the letting-in of a little light upon a doctrine which is, even at this day, cankering the lives of hundreds of thousands of our fellows, men, women, and children—especially the children—in different parts of the world. Where this terrible dogma does not embitter happiness, it corrupts character. Where people believe with a realized belief, their whole lives must be overshadowed with its stupendous horror ; where they only pretend to believe, the extent of their hypocrisy can be measured only by their pretence.

The task of preparing this little book has not been a pleasant one, and as it proceeded there have been moments when I have been compelled to lay aside my work—I have felt absolutely overwhelmed and sickened by the interminable repetition of ferocious exultations at the pain and sorrow supposed to await the majority of the human race, the nauseous imaginings, the inhumanity of man to man. I have, however, been encouraged to persevere in my task by the hope that these pages may help some here and there to realize the full and dreadful significance of the Christian hell ; and, realizing it, to reject it as a debasing and humiliating survival of an ignorant and superstitious past.

H. B. B.

October 1, 1913.

CHAPTER I

INTRODUCTION

Decline in Belief—Necessary for the Common People—New
Testament Teaching—Fate of Unbelievers—Exclusive Salvation—The Rich Man—Nature of Punishment—Church of
England — Farrar — Nonconformists—Salvation Army — Revivals—Missionaries—Roman Catholics—Education.

AMONG scholars and advanced thinkers there exists a
comfortable assumption that the idea of the devil and
hell has become "a negligible quantity"; that it is
not worth bothering about except as a matter of anti-
quarian research. It is a subject rarely discussed,
seldom even named, in polite society; and is considered rather an unseemly topic for the platform or
for general conversation. Contrasted with the wide-
spread terrorism of the past, this attitude is, indeed,
sufficiently remarkable, and if we looked no further
we might be led to believe that the days of hell as
a priestly incentive to morality have passed away.
Unfortunately for morality, this sanguine view is very
far from representing the real state of affairs.

It is true that during the last half century, among
certain classes of the community in England and
other progressive countries, there has been a notable
decline in the belief in hell as a place of punishment
for evildoers. Up to fifty years ago the Bible was
regularly read in nearly all middle-class families in
England and Scotland. It was read day by day,
chapter by chapter, from Genesis to Revelation; and

when the last chapter of Revelation was finished, the reader turned back and began at the first in Genesis once more. This practice, once universal, has now almost disappeared in large centres, but is still to be found among dwellers in small country towns and rural villages. Fifty years ago the Bible was looked upon as all-important for the instruction of the young in the schools, and in season and out of season it was hammered into the minds of the working classes. Religion, with its hopes and fears of rewards and punishments, was held necessary for women, children, and the common people.

Dr. Thomas Burnet (1635–1715), who opposed the doctrine of eternity of punishment in his Latin treatise *De Statu Mortuorum*, nevertheless enjoined: "Whatsoever you determine within yourself and in your own breast concerning these punishments, whether they are eternal or not, yet you ought to use the common doctrine and the common language when you preach or speak to the people, especially those of the lower rank who are ready to run headlong into vice and are to be restrained from evil by the fear of punishment." To this advice he puts a marginal note: "Whoever shall translate these sentiments [from the Latin in which he wrote] into our mother tongue, I shall think it was done with evil design and to bad purpose." Dr. Watts recklessly disregarded this injunction, and appended a translation as a note to Discourse 13 in his *World to Come.*

The Rev. J. Francis, preaching against Chartism in 1839, expressed the opinion that a firm belief in "a hell, where the wicked shall be eternally tormented," was a certain safeguard against political agitation (*Eternal Torment*, Lightfoot and Bradlaugh debate, p. 6).

Fifty years ago Herbert Spencer could write: "Even now, for the great mass of men, unable through lack of culture to trace out with due clearness those good and bad consequences which conduct brings round through the established order of the Unknowable, it is needful that there should be vividly depicted future torments and future joys—pains and pleasures of a definite kind, produced in a manner direct and simple enough to be clearly imagined. Nay, still more must be conceded. · Few if any are as yet fitted wholly to dispense with such conceptions as are current" (*First Principles*, chap. v, § 32).

"Theology," says Professor Bury, "has been regarded as a good instrument for keeping the poor in order, and unbelief as a cause or accompaniment of dangerous political opinions. The idea has not altogether disappeared that free thought is peculiarly indecent in the poor ; that it is highly desirable to keep them superstitious in order to keep them contented ; that they should be duly thankful for all the theological as well as social arrangements which have been made for them by their betters. I may quote from an essay of Mr. Frederic Harrison an anecdote which admirably expresses the becoming attitude of the poor towards ecclesiastical institutions. 'The master of a workhouse in Essex was once called in to act as chaplain to a dying pauper. The poor soul faintly murmured some hopes of heaven. But this the master abruptly cut short, and warned him to turn his last thoughts towards hell. "And thankful you ought to be," said he, "that you have a hell to go to "'" (*Freedom of Thought*, p. 222).

Before the disintegrating force of the "Higher Criticism" made itself felt, the authorized English version of the Bible was accepted by English-speaking people as true in its entirety ; every word of it was taken in its exact and literal meaning ; there was no selection of texts, no accepting of some and rejecting of others ; all were divinely inspired ; all were the direct utterance of an Almighty God. When, therefore, people read in Matthew xxv, 41, that the Lord

said " Depart from me, ye cursed, into everlasting fire,
prepared for the devil and his angels," they believed
the fire was a real fire, as real as and far more
powerful than that at which they warmed themselves
and cooked their food ; they believed that the devils
were evil-smelling monsters with hoof, horns, and tail—
restless and unappeasably malign.   The impression
they received from the Bible was strengthened and
enlarged by the teachings of the early Christian
Fathers and of noted contemporary divines, and even
more perhaps by the vivid descriptions drawn by
popular writers like Bunyan, whose *Sighs from Hell, or
the Groans of a Damned Soul* has gone through many
editions.   The poets also have had their full share in
making hell real to the believing Christian ; from
Cædmon to Milton the gloomy horrors of hell have
been an unfailing source of inspiration.   Indeed,
Dante and Milton between them are said to have
done more to make hell real to people than any
other writers, lay or clerical ; but that is an aspersion.

Many who reject the gross barbarism and brutality
of the Old Testament accept the New with unction.
Nevertheless, the appalling doctrine of eternal punishment which is the keystone to the New Testament
was unknown to the earlier Hebrews.   The New
Testament teaches everlasting punishment as a fate
which can be avoided neither by the unbeliever nor
the rich man, whatever chances of salvation may be
open to the rest :—

   Mark xvi, 16 : "He that believeth not shall be
damned."
   2 Thessalonians ii, 11, 12 : "......God shall send
them strong delusion, that they should believe a lie :
That they all might be damned who believed not the
truth."

The doctrine of exclusive salvation has been held

from the earliest ages by every Christian Church.[1] St. Ignatius (first and second centuries), in writing to the Church of Ephesus, says : " Do not err, my brethren ; ......if any should corrupt the faith of God by evil doctrine......such a one, being defiled, shall depart into fire unquenchable. Likewise he who heareth him."

"Without the Church no one is saved," said Origen. " No one cometh to salvation and eternal life except he who hath Christ for his head ; but no one can have Christ for his head except he that is in His body, the Church," was the verdict of St. Augustine. St. Fulgentius was, if possible, still more explicit : " Hold most firmly and doubt not that not only all pagans, but also all Jews, heretics, and schismatics who depart from this present life outside the Catholic Church, are about to go into eternal fire prepared for the devil and his angels." This was the view taken by most of the Fathers.

At the Reformation all parties accepted the definition of faith called the Athanasian Creed, and acted upon it. Luther taught that remission of sins and sanctification are obtained only within the Church. Calvin said : " Beyond the bosom of the Church no remission of sins is to be hoped for, nor any salvation." Luther and his adherents refused to hold communion with Zwingli and Œcolampadius, and both denounced the Socinians and Anabaptists. Calvin burned Servetus, and the Reformers of Holland expelled the Arminians not only from communion, but from their country. The British Churches have also insisted upon exclusive salvation ; the contrary doctrine, " that every man shall be saved by the law or sect which he

[1] Palmer's *Treatise on the Church of Christ* deals very fully with this subject.

professeth," was declared anathema by the Synod of London in 1562 ; and the Catechism of Dean Nowell, approved by various ecclesiastics in the time of Elizabeth, gives question and answer thus : " Is there hope of salvation outside the Church? Without it there is nothing but damnation, destruction, and perdition." The Saxon Confession presented to the Synod of Trent, 1551, the Helvetic Confession, the Belgic, the Scottish—all agree in consigning the unbeliever to hell. The " Westminster Confession " of the Presbyterian divines in 1647 declares that outside "the true religion......there is no ordinary possibility of salvation"; the Independents, and even the Quakers, avowed the same doctrine.

The case of the rich man is very little better than that of the heretic :—

> Mark xix, 24 ; Mark x, 25; Luke xviii, 25 : " It is easier for a camel to go through the eye of a needle than for a rich man to enter into the kingdom of God."
>
> Luke xvi, 22 : "......The beggar died, and was carried by the angels into Abraham's bosom ; the rich man also died, and was buried : and in hell he lift up his eyes, being in torments......But Abraham said, 'Son, remember that thou in thy lifetime receivedst thy good things, and likewise Lazarus evil things ; but now he is comforted, and thou art tormented.' "

According to these verses the only vice of the rich man is his wealth ; the only virtue of the poor man, his poverty.

The New Testament leaves no room for uncertainty as to the nature of the punishment which awaits the damned. Hell is described in Matt. v, 22, and xviii, 8 and 9, as a region of " fire "; in Mark ix, 43–48, as a " fire that shall never be quenched : where their worm dieth not "; in Mark ix, 49, as a place where

" everyone shall be salted with fire "; in Matt. xiii, 42 and 50, as a " furnace of fire [where] there shall be wailing and gnashing of teeth "; in Rev. xiv, 10, as a region of " fire and brimstone "; in Rev. xix, 20, as " a lake of fire, burning with brimstone "; Rev. xx, 10–15, as " the lake of fire and brimstone, where the beast and the false prophet are, and shall be tormented day and night for ever and ever......And whosoever was not found written in the book of life was cast into the lake of fire."

The Church of England is further committed to the doctrine of eternal torment through the Book of Common Prayer. The Athanasian Creed begins and ends with the threat that those who do not keep their faith whole and undefiled " shall perish everlastingly." The more enlightened among the clergy and the laity desire to get rid of or modify the Athanasian Creed, but there is a body of opinion powerfully represented in the English Church Union which declares that the Creed is true, and must be defended to the death.[1] In the Litany appeals are addressed to the "Good Lord " to preserve miserable sinners " from the crafts and assaults of the devil ; from thy wrath, and from everlasting damnation." The ferocious Commination Service dwells upon the most just judgment pronounced by God when he consigned sinners into the fire everlasting. The sick are not spared, for in the order for the Visitation of the Sick the minister is instructed to terrify the possibly dying person with talk about the accusing and condemning and the "fearful judgment." Even in the form of Solemnization of Matrimony "the dreadful day of judgment " is not overlooked. The Thirty-nine Articles, which it is commanded that no man may

---

[1] *Times*, November 18, 1909.

B

draw aside in any way, or take in any but the literal and grammatical sense, accept the Athanasian Creed as proved by Holy Scripture, and assert the descent of Christ into hell, and the "unspeakable comfort" to godly persons of predestination and election.

Officially, therefore, the Church of England expressly and repeatedly accepts the doctrine of everlasting punishment. But since the day when Archdeacon Farrar repudiated with all his force a doctrine so cruel and so horrible, Church of England Protestants have been gradually giving up a belief in a hell as a place of physical torment, although they retain the formulas in their religious books, and continue to recite them in their Churches, and to teach the doctrine to children and primitive peoples. Farrar's repudiation was no sudden or isolated abandonment; he merely gave deliberate and emphatic utterance to the long-smouldering revolt of enlightened humanity against the inhumanity of religious barbarism. In spite of their oaths, and in spite of ancient prohibitions, more and more are the divines of the Church becoming eager "to draw the Articles aside" and put their own interpretation and comment upon that which their common sense rejects.

> Archdeacon Farrar's declaration against eternal torment went by no means unchallenged. Dr. E. B. Pusey wrote a book of two or three hundred pages in which he exhaustively and conclusively proved that from the first century onwards everlasting punishment had been a part of Christian belief and teaching.

Nonconformists have followed, with more or less hesitation, the example set them by Churchmen. Generally speaking, they take a narrower view of their creed, and attach greater value to the literal meaning of the words of the New Testament and to the teachings of their predecessors than their Anglican co-religionists. There are some — nay, many—who altogether reject the doctrine of eternal torment; but there are also very many who continue to lay stress upon the horrors of hell. Nor can they do otherwise so long as they abide by the Westminster Confession, which allows no room for doubt. It distinctly says that "the wicked who know not God and obey not the Gospel of Jesus Christ shall be cast into eternal torments and be punished with everlasting destruction." To assert and maintain the contrary is denounced as "very pernicious, and to be detested." In the Larger Catechism, in answer to question sixty, it is affirmed "they who never having heard the Gospel, know not Jesus Christ, and believe not in time, cannot be saved, *be they never so diligent to frame their lives according to the light of nature, or the law of that religion which they profess.*" The Shorter Catechism, also agreed upon by the Westminster Assembly of 1647, and used in the schools of Scotland to-day, teaches that through the guilt of Adam's first sin all mankind fell under the wrath and curse of God, and became liable to the pains of hell for ever; that no mere man can keep free from sin, and every sin deserves God's wrath and curse both in this life and the life to come.[1]

Whole-hearted followers of Calvin naturally preach his doctrines of predestination and eternal punishment; even those who profess more liberal ideas cannot altogether rid themselves of hell and the devil. Take, for example, Pastor Thomas of Geneva, who has a considerable reputation outside his own Canton,

---

[1] Answers to Questions 19, 82, and 84.

and a fairly numerous following at home and abroad, especially in Holland, where the Queen Wilhelmina is his fervent protector and admirer. Pastor Thomas has no doubt about the existence of the devil. In a work entitled *Fictions ou Réalités*, published in 1903, he speaks of the power of Satan, saying that it is great but not infinite, and the day on which God wishes to destroy him he will do so at once. To represent the devil as a mere tool dependent on God's will and pleasure is apparently the best a twentieth-century professedly liberal Calvinist Protestant can do for humanity !

The Lutherans are in no better case. In February, 1909, eight of the Lutheran clergy of Sweden, including Bishop Lönegren, attended a meeting organized by the Stockholm Freethought Society for the purpose of advocating measures to enable the clergy to deny the existence of the devil, hell, and eternal damnation without being penalized. Seven out of the eight voted for retaining hell and the devil ; the eighth, Pastor Nils Hannerz, openly stated that among his religious conceptions there was no place for the devil, and later he wrote in an open letter, " I deny all belief in a devil." This outspoken declaration on the part of Pastor Hannerz was gravely considered at the Stockholm Konsistorium. During the discussion the chairman, Pastor Primarius Hähl, said : " We must stand by the Augsburg Confession; and we cannot deny Jesus's own words, for it is not in a few places and to a small extent only that He talks of the devil." His colleagues for the most part seemed to agree with him, although after several meetings and prolonged discussions they ended in acquitting Pastor Hannerz of unorthodoxy.[1]

[1] *Literary Guide*, March, 1910.

The Salvation Army, a body constantly and successfully appealing to the public for funds, owes its very existence to the doctrine of hell. It was born of eternal damnation ; it lives on blood and fire ; without hell there would be no salvation.

> The Orders and Regulations direct that persons who doubt the existence of " a real devil, a real hell," must not be recommended as candidates for officership. The officer has to see that his soldiers are supplied with "facts about heaven and hell," and must constantly seek to startle people with talk about death, the judgment day, and hell, " with its reproaches, upbraidings, and companionships ; its memories, its despair, and its duration." He is instructed that "the terrors of the law—that is, such subjects as sin, death, judgment, hell, and the like —will be found most useful to awaken sinners and bring them to repentance......These topics alarm and make men think and feel and seek mercy. The F. O.......must not take any notice of the objections of ignorant people about working on the feelings of sinners by trying to arouse their fears." In the Religious Trust Deed of the Army (1868), in which William Booth declared that the religious doctrines professed, believed, and taught " are and *shall ever be*" as therein laid down, the eleventh and last article runs : " We believe in the immortality of the soul ; in the resurrection of the body ; in the general judgment at the end of the world ; in the endless punishment of the wicked." This is repeated in the Articles of War as the eighth clause, and is the eleventh article of " The Doctrine of the Salvation Army" appended to the candidate's form of application for appointment as officer.

The Salvation Army not only makes the endless punishment of the wicked an article of belief to be held for " ever," but insists upon its officers continually dinning "its despair and its duration" into people's ears.

The great day of judgment, sin, and hell are the inspiration of every great revival movement ; they are also the master cards relied upon by the missionary in his none too successful gamble for the souls of enlightened Chinese and of ignorant and superstitious savages.

Missionaries, however, overrate the value of the fear of hell as a means of conversion. It may win over the timid and cowardly, but it repels the brave and loyal. It is told of Radbod, an old Scandinavian king, that after long resistance he finally consented to be baptized. He had put one foot in the water when he bethought himself to ask the priests if he should meet his forefathers in heaven. He was told no—that they, being unbaptized heathens, were eternally damned in hell. He thereupon drew back his foot, saying that he preferred to be in hell with his brave ancestors than in heaven with the Christian priests.[1] There are Radbods to be met with everywhere, wherever there are brave and loyal men.

Revivals are encouraged by wealthy Christians, and millions of pounds are subscribed every year by Christians of every denomination to support foreign missions. The subscribers may or may not believe in hell for themselves, but they cheerfully pay for this horrible doctrine to be taught to others. The subscribers should be under no illusion as to the use that is made of their money—in this respect at least—for the appeal is made to them expressly to save the soul of the heathen.

An American missionary, in a public address on his return from China, said : " Fifty thousand a day go down to the fire that is not quenched. Six hundred millions more are going the same road.

[1] Alger, *History of the Doctrine of a Future Life*, p. 342.

Should you not think at least once a day of the fifty thousand who that day sink to the doom of the lost!" The American Board of Commissioners of Foreign Missions declared that "To send the gospel to the heathen is a work of great exigency. Within the last thirty years a whole generation of five hundred millions have gone down to eternal death." In a tract issued by the Board, we find "The heathen are involved in the ruins of the apostasy, and are expressly doomed to perdition. Six hundred millions of deathless souls on the brink of hell! What a spectacle!"[1] The Rev. Sir G. W. Cox, in his *Life of Bishop Colenso*,[2] records the solemn protest made by Colenso against the prayer printed for the use of a missionary institution of the Church of England, which begins : " O Eternal God, Creator of all things, *mercifully remember* that the souls of unbelievers are' the work of Thy hands, and that they are created in Thy resemblance. Behold, O Lord, *how hell is filled with them* to the dishonour of Thy Holy Name."

Whatever waverings may be found in the real or nominal beliefs of non-Catholic Christians, there is no ambiguity whatever, and there never has been any ambiguity, in the teaching of the Church of Rome, by far the most numerous of all Christian bodies. Catholic authorities have differed as to whether the judgment of the dead takes place immediately after death or at some later period. Origen even ventured to suggest that after a period of suffering there would be an end to hell's torments ; but he was denounced for his heresy, and the Catholic Church has always made a hell of punishment for sinners an article of faith and a source of income. In this thirteenth year of the twentieth century we actually have a learned Professor of Theology (Herr Joseph Bautz) at the University of Munster publishing a book

---

[1] Alger, p. 545.   [2] Vol. i, p. 154.

upon hell, in which he explains that at the present time hell and its fire are not necessarily very extensive, since they are inhabited solely by spirits. "If after the resurrection of the body these dimensions are insufficient, the creator of the new abode will provide accordingly." And this is up-to-date teaching in enlightened and scientific Germany!

Since Protestantism happens to preponderate so overwhelmingly in Great Britain, Catholicism is comparatively quiet and unobtrusive, and consequently Rationalists are rather apt to ignore it. This is not altogether wise, for, although the Church of Rome may be quiet, it is not idle. Its active and persistent opposition to Secular Education met with some measure of success at the Trade Union Congress of 1912, and it avowedly seeks to gain an influence in the Labour movement. In Australasia and in Canada, where Catholicism is much stronger than in England, its influence is proportionately greater, and is used more openly and directly. The threat of withholding absolution for sin is a formidable lever when applied to a credulous people who believe that those who die in a state of mortal sin are doomed to the everlasting tortures of hell.

Protestant Christianity is to-day in the melting-pot. The Protestantism of sixty or seventy years ago is rapidly disappearing from the towns, if more slowly from the rural districts. The struggle of the future will be between the fullest assertion of the right of private judgment as it is found in Rationalism, and complete belief and submission to authority as we find it in the Church of Rome. That that Church has already gained sufficient power to turn the scale against Rationalism on the question of Secular Education in a congress of Labour men and women is sufficiently serious, and ought to be regarded as a warning.

Education in the Church schools under Protestantism has been irrational enough, as we know to our cost.

Among "the first lessons in reading and spelling" contained in a little book entitled *Little Albert's Primer*, and lately in use in the village schools of the south of England, we find such passages as " As for such as love not the way of the Lord, He will hide His face from them, and will not save them, but they shall go down to the pit." As for the boy who is naughty and takes "God's name in vain, he will come to an ill end if he be not well whipped at school and at home, day and night." On the cover at the back is a " child's evening hymn," of which the second verse begins thus :—

> But how my childhood runs to waste,
> My sins, how great their sum.

Bad as this is, it is enlightened compared with the education which has existed in such Catholic countries as Spain and Portugal. Rationalists are striving to win definite moral instruction for the children in the schools, but so long as the doctrine of "the pit," the "ill end," "the wrath to come," and " sin " is taught, there can be no true moral training. Fear is the foundation upon which the priest insists that character must be built up, and never yet has a true and stable morality been built upon the quicksands of fear.

CHAPTER II

LITERATURE AND ICONOGRAPHY

Extensive and Repulsive—Illuminated MSS.—Hone's *Ancient Mysteries*—Wall Paintings—Stained Windows—Sculpture—Church Furniture.

THE literature of hell is enormous, and is as repulsive as it is vast. Thousands of more or less lengthy treatises and sermons have been written upon the punishment of sinners in hell. Probably no subject has a more copious bibliography, unless, perchance, it is the subject of heaven. And if the descriptions of the torments of the damned are not more numerous than the descriptions of the bliss of the saints, they are as a rule far more impressive, far more popular. For one who has read Dante's *Paradiso* and Milton's *Paradise Regained*, there are hundreds who are more or less familiar with the *Inferno* and the *Paradise Lost*. Tales of bliss quickly cloy the imagination ; there are very few who are not soon weary of descriptions of unrelieved joy. It is true that the frequent repetition of tales of terror after a time cease to terrify, but he must be callous indeed who does not feel a thrill of pain in picturing that

habitation, fraught with fire,
Unquenchable, the house of woe and pain,[1]

[1] *Paradise Lost*, end of Bk. VI.

that city of " eternal pain " whose gates shut out all hope.[1]

Poets and priests of every creed have written more or less detailed descriptions of the hell or underworld to which they commit their personal enemies, and those who for one reason or another they class as sinners ; and each writer in turn has put forward his own dreadful conception as substantially accurate.

Not only is there an extensive literature of hell, but the early pictures also are both numerous and ghastly. The present generation is familiar with a pictured hell mainly through Doré's illustrations to the *Divina Commedia*, and in these there is always the beauty of line, or shade, or grouping which shines through the ugliness of the scenes which the artist depicts. But the old pictures have scarcely a redeeming point, except when, as frequently happens, the faces of the tortured victims wear a cheerful and reassuring smile. Pictures of the devil and hell's torments date from very early times, for it was customary to adorn the illuminated service missals, the psalters, poems, and text-books with more or less artistic representations of the devil and the final punishment of the wicked.

In order to keep this book within the narrow limits assigned to it, the literature and iconography here dealt with are, with very few exceptions, confined to those books which have appeared in England, either as translations in general circulation, or originally written in English, and those illustrations which are to be found on or in English buildings or in English books.

Some of the earliest English pictorial representations available to-day are those attached to Cædmon's *Metrical Paraphrase of Scripture History*, and belong

---

[1] " Lasciate ogni speranza, voi ch'entrate " (*Inferno*, c. 3, l. 9.)

Fig. 1.—The Temptation. (Cædmon's *Paraphrase*, tenth
century.) From the Archælogia, vol. 24.

to the later part of the tenth century.   Fig. 1 shows
the messenger of the bound Satan sent forth to tempt
Eve and his appearance before her in the form of a
serpent.   Fig. 2 shows the cursing of the serpent as

Fig. 2.—The Almighty Cursing the Serpent.   (Cædmon's *Para-phrase*, tenth century.)   From the Àrchælogia, vol. 24.

related in Genesis iii, 14.   Fig. 3 belongs to the
late twelfth century,[1] and depicts St. Guthlac of

[1] Harley Roll ; British Museum.

Croyland at the mouth of hell receiving a whip from
St. Bartholomew. St. Guthlac is generally represented as scourging demons or being tormented by
them. In the thirteenth century, a text-book was
compiled by a friar named Raymond at the command
of Gregory IX, who furthered ordered that this book,

Fig. 3.—St. Guthlac Tormented by Devils and Receiving a
Whip from St. Bartholomew. (Twelfth century.)
From Harley Roll, British Museum.

known as *Gregory's Decretals*, should be used by the
doctors of law in the schools of the time. A copy,
now in the British Museum, was made in due course
for the Priory of St. Bartholomew, and is lavishly
ornamented with pictures which form valuable material
as to the manners and ideas of the period. The

Fig. 4.—Satan Overcome by the Virgin. (*Gregory's Decretals*, thirteenth century.)

Fig. 5.—Satan Yielding up a Soul to the Virgin. (*Gregory's Decretals*, thirteenth century.)

monks are frequently represented as corrupt, but after having sown their wild oats they usually repent, become holy men, and go to heaven. Figs. 4 and 5 are both taken from the Bartholomew copy of *Gregory's Decretals.* Fig. 4 represents Satan, who has issued from hell-mouth and been battering the gates of heaven, overcome by the Virgin. In Fig. 5 Satan is giving up a soul to the Virgin in the presence of its guardian angel. Fig. 6 belongs to the early fourteenth century, and was reproduced in Hone's *Ancient Mysteries* from the original copper-plate engraved by Michael Burgers for Hearne, the antiquary. It is supposed to depict Christ's descent into hell (generally known as the "Harrowing of Hell"), as related in the Apocryphal Gospel of Nicodemus :—

> XVI, 19 : The mighty Lord appeared in the form of a man. 20 : And with his invincible power visited those who sat in the deep darkness by iniquity, and the shadow of death by sin.
>
> XVII, 13 : Then the king of glory, trampling upon death, seized the prince of hell, deprived him of all his power.
>
> XIX, 12 : And taking hold of Adam by his right hand, he ascended from hell, and all the saints of God followed him.

Hone reproduces also a wood-cut (Fig. 7) from a rare German work of 1506, showing a sinner bound to the devil's tail. This, he considered, stands alone as a form of infernal punishment.

It will be easily understood that the persons who had access to these wonderful monuments of monkish skill and ingenuity, the illuminated MSS., were comparatively few in number; and as it was most important that the common folk should be fully instructed in the nature of the punishments which awaited evil-doers in the next world, it was a very

Fig 6.—The Harrowing of Hell. (Fourteenth century.) From Hone's *Ancient Mysteries.*

common custom to paint representations of the day of
judgment on the wall of the church, usually over the
chancel arch, but sometimes on the west wall, and less
often on one of the others.   Within recent times
there were still a hundred of these doom wall paintings in existence in English churches.   Of some of

Fig. 7.—Sinner Bound to Devil's Tail.   (Sixteenth century.)
From Hone's *Ancient Mysteries.*

these there are now only the barest traces left: others
which were long hidden under a thick coat of whitewash are in a fair state of preservation.   The
example (Fig. 8) of these wall paintings given here is
from Chaldon Church, Surrey, and is one of the

Fig. 8.—The Ladder of the Soul's Salvation; Chaldon Church, Surrey. (Twelfth century.)

C 2

earliest as well as the most perfect now existing. Having seen it, one learns without surprise that in some cases where the process of cleaning the church walls has revealed one of these doom pictures it has been quickly hidden under whitewash once again. The authorities clearly felt that these early representations of the torments of the wicked were more likely to excite hilarity than fear in the minds of people to-day.

The particular subject of the wall painting in Chaldon Church dates from the last decade of the twelfth century, and is unique in England.[1] It is known as the "Ladder of the Soul's Salvation." In the centre of the painting is the ladder with a vision of God set in a circle at the top. The ladder and a horizontal bar of ornament divide the picture into four sections. In that at the lower left hand a great cauldron over a fire occupies the chief place, in which a batch of souls is being stirred up by two great demons. Other demons are busy tormenting other souls ; one lying on his back is biting the feet of three little figures, said to represent girls who were too fond of dancing ; a dog is biting the hand of a woman who gave food to the dogs which she should have given to the poor ; a soul with a bottle is punished for drunkenness. Next to the ladder is another big demon with a two-pronged fork picking off souls as they try to climb upwards ; behind him are a man and woman holding between them a horn, the woman with a piece of money in her open hand. In the bottom compartment on the right are two demons holding the bridge of spikes (so prominent a feature in the Zoroastrian and Mohammedan religions), across which five souls are trying to pass : one, a man, holds a bowl

[1] See the *Victoria History of Surrey*, Vol. IV.

of milk, two women hold a ball of wool and some
uncarded flax, the fourth carries a pick, and the fifth
a blacksmith's tools.   Beneath the bridge sits a usurer
in the flames, with money bags tied round him, vomiting and catching gold coins.   On either side of him
evil spirits are tempting couples to illicit affections.
On the extreme right is the tree of knowledge, with
the serpent entwined in the upper branches.   Above,

Fig. 9.—St. Dunstan and the Devil.   Bodleian Library.

on the right, there is a representation of the " harrowing of hell," and of an angel assisting two souls,
popularly supposed to be Enoch and Elijah, who went
to heaven by an unusual road.   On the left are
St. Michael weighing souls and Satan trying to weigh
down the scale.   It will be observed that in this
" Ladder of Salvation " the artist has devoted by far
the greater part of his picture to damnation, and

allotted very small space to salvation.   In a pamphlet
issued by the rector of Chaldon it is claimed that after
a little explanation and study the painting will be
found full of teaching both in the way of encourage-
ment and warning.

In some churches instead of wall paintings there
are stained windows representing the last judgment
and the torture of the damned.   These windows are
quite common in Catholic countries, but are comparatively rare in England, although there are some, both

Fig. 10.—Hell Mouth ; Lincoln Cathedral.
(Eleventh century.)

ancient and modern.   There is a very elaborate
window dating from the last year of the fifteenth
century at Fairford Church in Gloucestershire.
Fig. 9 belongs to a later period ; it is from one of
the windows of the Bodleian Library, and represents
the temptation of St. Dunstan, an English archbishop
of the tenth century.   St. Dunstan was patron saint
of the goldsmiths, and was himself a worker in gold.
According to tradition, when he was expelled from

Court he retired to a hermitage near Glastonbury Church, where in the intervals of prayer and other religious exercises he worked at his craft. On one occasion the devil (devils seem to abound in the vicinity of churches!) came to gossip with him. St. Dunstan went on talking until his tongs were red hot, when he turned suddenly and caught the unsuspecting devil by the nose, and, holding him howling there, calmly upbraided him for his wickedness.

Fig. 11.—*Miserere* Seat Carving ; Ludlow.   (Fourteenth century.)

Representations of hell in sculpture are also rare in England, although very common and sometimes very elaborate in the churches on the Continent. The accompanying hell mouth (Fig. 10) dates from the eleventh century, and is from the frieze on the west front of Lincoln Cathedral.

The devil and judgment scenes are also to be

found in the carvings of abbey and cathedral furniture; more especially on the fonts and on the *miserere* seats in the choir stalls.   An interesting early bas-relief (probably seventh century) on the font of East Meon Church, Hampshire, represents Eve as giving the apple to the serpent.   Fig. 11 is taken from a *miserere* seat at Ludlow and represents a naked ale-wife, with her characteristic headdress, being dragged off to hell by a headless demon for having used false measures, while another demon plays the bagpipes; and a third, the accuser, jubilantly reads the list of her sins from a long roll.

CHAPTER III

THE SURPASSING HORROR OF THE
CHRISTIAN IDEA

Not Original—Eastern Origin—Northern Ideas—Locality of
Hell: the Sun, the Moon, the Interior of the Earth—The
Worst Punishments for Unbelievers—Doctrines Peculiar to
Christianity: (1) The Absolute Eternity of Punishment;
(2) The "Winsome Joy" Felt by the Saints in Watching
the Tortures of the Damned; (3) The Damnation of Infants.

ALTHOUGH a hell of punishment for sinners has been
regarded as so essential a part of Christianity that
Justin Martyr declared that if there was no hell there
was no God,[1] and Chrysostom said that it is because
God is good that he has prepared a hell,[2] nevertheless
the Christian hell is in no sense an original conception. It is merely an intensification of the later
classic hell, which was itself a graft of Eastern origin.

We find the earliest traces of the idea in the
account of the descent of Ishtar, the Babylonian
Venus, into the land of No-return, in search of her
lover Tammuz; and more vividly in the nightly
descent of the Egyptian Sun God and the journey of
the souls with him through the underworld, the terrors
overcome, the weighing of souls before Osiris, the
judgment, and the punishment of the wicked. We
may trace it in the awful torments of the souls of the
Hindu dead, the ghastly horrors of the later (corrupt)

[1] *Second Apology for the Christians*, § 9.
[2] *Epistle to Philemon*, Hom. 3.

31

Buddhist hells, and the Zoroastrian punishment of the accursed. The earliest hells, however, were not places of punishment ; they were, like Sheol, abodes of the more or less silent dead, "where the wicked cease from troubling and the weary are at rest."

Virgil's hell lasted a thousand years ; the Christian hell endures for ever and ever. Pluto became transformed into Satan, the Furies became demons, Hades was replaced by the bottomless pit, and the fiery river Phlegethon turned into the lake of brimstone and fire.

The early Fathers were quite aware of the existence of other hells. Tertullian, in his *Apology Against the Heathen* (c. 198), says : "We are laughed at when we preach that God shall judge the world, for so do all the poets also, and the philosophers feign a judgment-seat in the shades below ; and if we threaten men with hell, which is a storehouse of hidden fire beneath the earth, for the punishing of men, we are forthwith borne down by jeers, for so also is there a river called Pyriphlegethon." Tertullian's explanation is that the poets and philosophers derived their doctrines from "our mysteries"—*i.e.*, the earlier derived from the later.

To the Eastern conception of heat was added cold —the great dread of the Northern nations. This is especially marked in the early English descriptions, and is consequently of peculiar interest to English-speaking peoples. From the fifth to the eleventh century there was considerable intercourse between the people of Denmark and Norway and the Anglo-Saxons, as others called them, or the English folk, as they called themselves. There was even a tradition that the Danish hero Scyld had floated in from the sea to become the ancestor of the English and the Danes. To a large extent the gods of the Northmen were the gods of the English ; they believed in Odin, the All Father, who lives from ever-lasting to everlasting, governing all things, great and small ; and from Hel, the Norse goddess of death, we get the name, and a great deal more than the name, of the Christian abode of the damned. Whether the Northmen or the early English had any belief in the immortality of the soul is extremely doubtful. "The secrets of life are known to us only for a short space," said the Thegn at Godmanham ; "what has gone before, what shall follow after, we cannot tell."[1] When the English were converted to Christianity they became imbued with the sure and certain fear of eternal torment ; and with the Norse idea of Niflheim, the place of mist and cold, they blended the New Testament teaching of a hell of fire.

The poets who wrote the *Historical Paraphrase of the Scriptures* (long ascribed to Cædmon, and even now generally referred to under his name) picture hell as an abyss of mingled heat and cold in the nether world of the north ; so deep that it seems 100,000 miles from the bottom to Hellgate. They describe it as a dire, loathly, woeful, dim abode ; a windy, accursed hall ; a bitter ground, containing a tumultuous sea of poisonous fire surrounded by lofty nesses, beneath which the devils lament and mourn without hope ; a place of serpents, adders, dragons, and demons howling in their misery ; where light never comes, where all is gloomy horror, and where naked men struggle with worms (Fig. 12). The gnashing of teeth of those in torment may be heard for twelve miles without the gate, beside which dragons breathing out flame dwell eternally. The whole pit rages with fire and venom, and, when Satan speaks, the words fly from his lips in venomous sparks (*National Life in Early English Literature*, E. Dale, M.A., D.Litt., p. 101). The early English conception

---

[1] The year 627. Bede. II. 13.

of hell was also, like the Egyptian, closely associated with the setting sun. " Tell me," says an Anglo-Saxon dialogue,[1] " why is the sun red at even ? " " I tell thee because she looketh down upon hell ! " is the reply. This idea was revived at the close of the

Fig. 12.—Naked Men Struggling with Worms.   Hellewite.

eighteenth century by Tobias Swinden, Rector of Cuxton, in Kent, who published a book in which he sought to show that the sun was hell, and the spots on the sun gatherings of damned

[1] Thorpe's *Analecta Anglo-Saxonica.*

souls. Martin Tupper, on the other hand, placed hell in the moon :—

> I know thee well, O Moon, thou caverned realm,
> Sad Satellite, thou giant ash of death ;
> Blot on God's firmament, pale home of crime,
> Scarr'd prison-house of sin, where damned souls
> Feed upon punishment. Oh ! thought sublime,
> That amid night's black deeds, when evil prowls
> Through the broad world, thou, watching sinners well,
> Glarest o'er all, the wakeful eye of—Hell !

In the folk-lore of Russia and North Germany the moon frequently figures as the place of punishment.[1] The world is indebted to the learned Jesuit Father Hardouin (1646–1729) for one of the most extraordinary theories concerning the locality of hell. The interior of the earth, he said, is filled with the fires of hell, and in order to escape the eternal flames the damned are everlastingly trying to climb the inner crust of the earth, which is the wall of hell. Their weight causes the earth to turn, just as a squirrel turns his cage, or a dog turns the spit. This is the explanation of the rotation of the earth.[2]

In all religions, without exception, the performance of religious rites and ceremonies rather than virtuous deeds is rewarded, and the punishment of immorality is invariably less than the punishment of unbelief. Those who are classed as perfectly bad, who suffer the worst and most horrible torments, are the unbelievers ; unbelief is always the great crime. For every other sin repentance may be possible, but without faith there is absolutely no salvation. If religions are true (and any argument which is held to prove one may be used with equal effect of any

[1] Farrar's *Paganism and Christianity*, p. 126.
[2] Delepierre's *L'Enfer*, p. 125. Hardouin wrote several works, which were condemned by the Jesuit Order in France and prohibited by the *Index Congregation* there, although not in Spain (*Putnam's Censorship*, Vol. II, p. 42).

other), unless men believe them all, they are bound after death to be punished in all the hells except their own ; and those who believe that none of the religions are true have only to go to one more hell than the rest. What is one more hell among so many, compared with the peace of mind which unbelief brings during life ?

But, although a hell of some kind or another is common to all religions, and they all exhibit marked similarities in the nature of the punishment allotted to sinners after death, there are three important particulars in which the Christian hell differs from every other, and in these Christianity reached a pinnacle of ferocity and moral insensibility never attained before or since in any religion known to mankind.

The three points in which Christianity thus stands out from other religions is in (1) the doctrine of the absolute eternity of punishment, (2) the joy felt by the blessed at the sight of the torments of the damned, and (3) the damnation of infants.

1. The hopelessness of eternal punishment.

Once damned, the agony of the sufferer is absolutely without hope. This eternity of unrelieved anguish and crushing despair is insisted upon with sickening reiteration by all theologians, with very few exceptions, until the latter half of last century. Many a Christian must have echoed the bitter cry of Marlowe's *Dr. Faustus* :—

> Oh ! if my soul must suffer for my sin,
> Impose some end to my incessant pain !
> Let Faustus live in hell a thousand years—
> A hundred thousand—and at last be saved.

But few indeed were those who ventured to foretell a termination to this incessant pain. Origen and some others, whose humanity compelled them to believe in the ultimate restoration of even the worst of sinners to heaven, were denounced as heretics.

2. The bliss felt by the saints in watching the tortures of the damned.

Psalms ii, 4.—He that sitteth in the heavens shall laugh ; the Lord shall have them in derision.

Proverbs i, 26–29.—I also will laugh at your calamity : I will mock when your fear cometh ;

When your fear cometh as a desolation, and your destruction cometh as a whirlwind, when distress and anguish cometh upon you.

Then shall they call upon me, but I will not answer ; they shall seek me early, but they shall not find me :

For that they hated knowledge, and did not choose the fear of the Lord.

Thomas Aquinas says : "That the saints may enjoy their beatitude and the grace of God more richly, a perfect sight of the punishment of the damned is granted them."[1]

Cynewulf, a poet of the eighth century, who has been called "the poet of the Cross," and his poem, *The Christ*, "the epic of salvation," describes the great joy felt by the righteous in regarding the sufferings of the damned : " In the vale of darkness the happy host see the damned suffering pain as a punishment for their sins, the surging flame, and biting of the serpents with bitter jaws—a school of burning creatures. From that sight waxes for them a winsome joy, when they see the others enduring the evil that they escaped through the mercy of the Lord."[2]

---

[1] *Summa*, Par III.
[2] Dale, *National Life in Early English Literature*, pp. 119, 121.

"When thou art scorching in thy flames," wrote Christopher Love, "when thou art howling in thy torments, then God shall laugh, and his saints shall sing and rejoice, that His power and wrath are thus made known to thee."

Bunyan, in his *World to Come*, is no less emphatic: "The saints shall rejoice that we are damned, and God is glorified in our destruction."

Jonathan Edwards devotes the greater part of a sermon[1] to demonstrate that "the sight of hell's torments will exalt the happiness of the saints for ever." The divine perfections require such punishments. By them the grace of God is glorified: "Every time they [the saints in heaven] look down upon the damned it will excite in them a lively and admiring sense of the grace of God in making them so to differ."

Samuel Hopkins simply revels in representing God and the saints as the most atrocious fiends. What could be more diabolical than this?—"The smoke of their torments shall ascend up in the sight of the blessed for ever and ever, and serve as a most clear glass always before their eyes, to give them a bright and most affecting view. This display of the Divine character will be most entertaining to all who love God, will give them the highest and most ineffable pleasure. Should the fire of this eternal punishment cease, it would in a great measure obscure the light of heaven, and put an end to the greater part of the happiness and glory of the blessed."[2]

Joachim Böldicke, a German writer of the eighteenth century, maintains that "the eternal torments of the damned spring from the pure benevolence of the

---

[1] *The Eternity of Hell's Torments.*
[2] Alger, p. 541.

deity, because the happiness of the elect will be so greatly heightened and intensified by the contemplation of their sufferings."

In his *Glimpse of Glory*, published in 1721 and republished by the Religious Tract Society in 1839, Andrew Wellwood, in describing the bliss of the saints, says: " Our Well-beloved has made our state every way excellent and glorious......That it might be wanting nothing of the top, and flower, and perfection of glory and exaltation, we have you [wicked men and devils] for a footstool, for ever to trample upon : all things are ours and for our honour and glory." " The beholding of the smoke of their torments is a surpassing delectation."

In a letter to the *Times*, dated August 8, 1905, the writer alleges that " the glory of God is in the punishment of the faithless."

3. The damnation of infants.

This was held to be the logical consequence of the doctrine set forth by Paul in Romans v, 12, that through Adam's fall a burden of sin rested upon all men, dooming them, without exception, to eternal punishment. They could escape this dire decree only through baptism.

St. Augustine (fourth century) taught that baptism was necessary to free the soul from the power which the devil had over it on account of Adam's sin, and that without baptism all were doomed to hell. He admitted that the crying of a baby is not sinful, and therefore does not deserve eternal damnation. In the Pelagian controversy, Julian the Pelagian objected that, if the doctrine of original sin were true, it were a cruel and wicked thing to beget children who would be born in a state of condemnation. To this St. Augustine replied (*Contra Julianum*, c. viii) that God

D

is the author of being to all men, many of whom will be eternally condemned, yet God is not to be accused of cruelty for creating them. He suggests that unbaptized infants who have only original sin, and are not loaded with sins of their own, may suffer a gentler condemnation than the personally guilty. Elsewhere (*De Verbis Apostoli*, serm. 14) in the same controversy he takes a less merciful view, saying: "I have explained to you what is the kingdom and what everlasting fire, so that when you confess the infant will not be in 'the kingdom,' you must acknowledge he will be in 'everlasting fire.'"[1]

St. Fulgentius (sixth century), in his treatise *De Fide*, writes: "Be assured, and doubt not, that not only men who have obtained the use of their reason, but also little children who have begun to live in their mothers' womb and have there died, or who, having been just born, have passed away from the world without the sacrament of holy baptism administered in the name of the Father, Son, and Holy Ghost, must be punished by the eternal torture of undying fire; for, although they have committed no sin by their own will, they have, nevertheless, drawn with them the condemnation of original sin by their carnal conception and nativity."

Pope Gregory (seventh century) declared that those taken from their present life and not having the sacrament of salvation for their deliverance from original sin, though they have done nothing of their own here, yet there they undergo eternal torments.[2]

It is related in the vision of Alberico (1123) that when he, a boy of ten, made a visit to purgatory, personally conducted by St. Peter and two angels, he was startled to see one-year-old babes boiling in fiery

---

[1] Wall's *Infant Baptism*, Part II, c. vi, § 5.   [2] *Ibid*, § 6.

vapours. St. Peter thereupon explained to him that even a child a day old is not without sin, for in stretching out his arm to his mother he may strike her on the face !

One sect, known as the Hieracites, taught that no infant dying before the use of reason could possibly come to the kingdom of heaven. They held that marriage and begetting children was unlawful under the New Testament, and no married persons could inherit the kingdom of God.[1]

The belief in the damnation of unbaptized infants was generally held during the first eleven centuries of the Christian era,[2] but by degrees there grew up some abatement in the rigour which would consign helpless infants to eternal torment, and in the twelfth century a distinction was made between the punishment of original sin and actual sin. For original sin the penalty was deprivation of the sight of God ; for actual sin, the torments of everlasting hell. This led to the invention of a *limbus infantium* or *parvulorum* (or *infernus puerorum*), where unbaptized infants suffer no other torment than loss of heaven. Henceforward to assert the contrary was esteemed a heresy, and this doctrine of a *limbus infantium* is still held by the Catholic Church.[3]

The doctrine of the damnation of infants was by no means confined to the Roman Catholics. Wickliffe (1324–84) finds it hard to positively assert that the unbaptized infants of believers will be damned, but he says (*Trialog.*, c. iv) : "God, if He will, may damn such an infant and do him no wrong, and if He will he can save him......I know that whatever God does in it will be just and a work of mercy to be praised

---

[1] Wall, Part I, c. xxi, § 5.   [2] c. xxii, § 1.
[3] *Catholic Encyclopædia*, Art. " Hell."

of all the faithful." If infants *are* damned, then, he believes, they will suffer not only loss of heaven, but sensible punishment.[1] The Hussites of Bohemia hoped that infants dying unbaptized might be saved by the mercy of God in accepting their parents' faithful desire of baptizing for the deed. This hope of mercy for the innocent was denounced as a heresy, and formed part of the accusation against Huss.[2] Upon the Reformation Protestants generally held that the punishment of original sin is, in strictness, damnation in hell. Luther and his followers lay so much stress upon the necessity of the purge of baptism as to permit a layman to do it in cases of emergency, rather than that the infant should die without. Calvin and his adherents went a little further, and taught that unbaptized infants might be saved, provided the miss of baptism happened by no contumacy or neglect of the parent.[3]

From time to time protests have been raised against this fiendish doctrine of the eternal damnation of helpless infants. Zwingli was violently attacked because he ventured to exclude Christian infants from the penalty of original sin. A protest written by Antonius Cornelius, and published by Wechel in 1531, aroused the anger of a Catholic priest, Father Garasse, to such an extent that he denounced Cornelius in elegant language as "an abortion of hell," and rejoicingly tells how by divine judgment the publisher Wechel was reduced to poverty in consequence of having published this book.[4]

In 1690 a Quaker, named George Keith, objected not only to the damnation of infants, but to that

---

[1] Wall. II, c. vi, § 6.   [·] *Ibid.*
[3] *Ibid.*, c. vi, § 8.   [4] Alger, p. 954.

of heretics also, and was formally repudiated for
his humanity by "the ministers of the Gospel
in Boston." These ministers issued a book, the
preface of which is signed by four names :—"James
Allen, Joshuah Moody, Samuel Willard, and Cotton
Mather," in which they maintained the principles of
the Protestant religion against Keith's "calumnies."[1]
Taking it altogether, there has been small tenderness or
pity shown for the little ones by those who believed in
hell. Catholic and Calvinist have made infant damnation an integral part of their faith. The Puritans were, if
possible, more extreme than the Catholics. "Learn,"
wrote that awful Puritan priest, Christopher Love,
"that little children and young infants, though they
live but for a day, are in as great danger as men
that live a hundred years." People in their blind
conceit, he went on, call a child innocent; yet,
though they live but a minute in this world, God
may justly punish them for the sin of their nature.
The Bishop of Toronto, in the middle of last
century, published a declaration that "every child
of humanity, except the Virgin Mary, is from the
first moment of conception a child of wrath, hated
by the blessed Trinity, belonging to Satan, and
doomed to hell";[2] while the Rev. Dr. Nehemiah
Adams, a Congregational preacher of Boston, contemporary with the Bishop, had no hesitation
in suggesting that "the forty-two children that
mocked Elisha are now in hell."[3] For calling
Elisha "baldhead" the children are first devoured
by she-bears, and then consigned to everlasting
torment! Dr. Nathaniel Emmons, pastor of Franklin

[1] Alger, p. 955.   [2] Alger, p. 515.
[3] *Friends of Christ.* Sermon on "The Children in the
Temple."

Church, Mass., in a long sermon on the depravity of children,[1] contended that little children are moral agents before they are capable of uttering a single word, hence they are capable of sinning; they are, for example, capable of selfishness! In support of his contention he quotes, "thou wast a transgressor from the womb." Some divines have argued there is no salvation without faith, but infants cannot believe, therefore they cannot be saved; they are incapable of evil, therefore they cannot be damned; hence annihilation is the only future possible. But what are we to think of this? "Reprobate infants are vipers of vengeance which Jehovah will hold over hell with the tongs of wrath till they writhe up and cast their venom in his face"![2]

The Church of England forbids the ordinary office of burial to be used for an unbaptized infant, and within the recollection of the present generation it was customary, in some rural districts at least, to bury such children by night in a waste corner of the churchyard.

This kindly Christian doctrine of the damnation of unbaptized children gave rise in the Middle Ages to all sorts of legends. The *ignes fatui*, so often seen hovering about marshy or misty places, which science teaches the Rationalist are nothing more extraordinary than exhalations of "marsh gas," our superstitious forefathers imagined were the souls of unbaptized children endeavouring to guide travellers to the nearest water. In some districts there were legends of a spectral pack of "hell hounds," the souls of unbaptized children who could not rest, but roamed, and moaned, and shrieked through the woods all night. There is also the myth of the

[1] *Works*, Vol. IV.   [2] Alger, p. 536.

pitiful robin, whose little breast became burned and red through carrying drops of water in its bill to hell to relieve the suffering children there. In the border counties of England and in north-east Scotland the belief long prevailed that the souls of little children who died unbaptized wandered about in the air, restless and unhappy, until Judgment Day. In Northumberland it was customary to bury an unbaptized babe at the feet of an adult Christian corpse. In Ireland, in the sixteenth century, the right arms of male children were left unchristened in order that they might be able to give a more deadly blow. In the islands of Greece the peasantry still believe that stillborn children, or children who die unbaptized are in danger of becoming were-wolves and vampires.

CHAPTER IV

THE EARLY CHRISTIAN FATHERS

St. Ignatius—Justin Martyr—St. Theophilus—Tertullian—St. Hippolytus—St. Cyprian—Eusebius—St. Cyril—St. Basil—St. Chrysostom—St. Augustine—St. Gregory Nanzianzen—St. Jerome—Cyril of Alexandria.

THE teachings of the early Fathers of the Christian Church naturally had enormous influence in shaping future thought. That they had very definite ideas as to the everlasting punishment of sinners in hell may be gathered from the following brief extracts from their writings, taken, unless otherwise stated, from the crowd of witnesses cited by Dr. Pusey in his reply to Dr. Farrar[1] :—

St. Ignatius (first and second centuries) taught that he who corrupts the faith of God by evil teaching shall go into unquenchable fire, "and in like way *he who heareth him.*"[2]

An ancient Homily ascribed to Clement (c. 120–150) says that "Nothing shall deliver us from eternal punishment if we should disobey His commands." When the righteous behold those who have done amiss punished with grievous torments in unquenchable fire they shall give glory to God.[3]

Justin Martyr, in his *Second Apology for the Christians,* written about 160, speaks of those philo-

---

[1] *What is Faith as to Everlasting Punishment?* 3rd edition.
[2] P. 173.   [3] P. 177.

sophers who declare "that what we say about the wicked being punished in eternal fire is a mere boast and a bugbear; that it is through fear and not for the sake of what is good and pleasurable that we would have men live virtuously. I will reply briefly to this, that *if it be not so there is no God;* or if there is one He cares not for men; virtue and vice."[1] Justin Martyr did not mince matters; it was clear to him that belief in God necessitates belief in hell.

St. Theophilus, sixth Bishop of Antioch (c. 168), announced that there shall be anger, wrath, tribulation, and anguish, and at the last everlasting fire, for "the unbelieving and despisers" and others.[2]

Tertullian, in his *Apology against the Heathen* (c. 198), is very positive as to the eternal fire in which the wicked shall receive punishment; it is a fire which "consumeth not that which it burneth, but reneweth while it destroyeth." He says there are mountains ever burning which yet endure, and claims these as "a witness of the eternal fire, an example of that everlasting judgment which feedeth its own pains."[3] In describing the *Christian joys and spectacles* he dwells fondly upon the delights of the last and eternal Day of Judgment. With ferocious joy he tells how he shall wonder, laugh, rejoice, exult at beholding so many kings and others groaning together in the lowest darkness; the rulers and persecutors of the Name of the Lord melting amid insulting fires; those wise philosophers burning with their own disciples whom they had persuaded either that they had no souls, or that they would not return to their former bodies; the poets, too, trembling before the judgment seat of the

[1] Translation published by Frowde, 1861.   § 9.
[2] P. 187.
[3] *Tertullian.*   Translation by Rev. C. Dodgson, p. 101.

unlooked-for Christ. The tragic actors, the players, the wrestlers—all may be viewed in the fire. We can through faith see them even now in the imagination of the spirit, and thus have greater joys than from the circus, the theatre, and the race-course.[1]

St. Hippolytus, Bishop of Portus (second and third centuries), speaks of "the boiling flood of heaven's lake of fire" and "the worm that ceaselessly coils for food round the body."[2]

St. Cyprian declares that those who do not believe will be accursed and suffer a devouring punishment of lively flames, without repose or end.[3]

In the Clementine Homilies it is intimated that the soul even of the wicked is incorruptible, and suffers endless torture in unquenchable fire, and, never dying, receives no end to its misery.[4]

Eusebius (third and fourth centuries) says that they who set at naught the saving grace shall lie in hell like sheep and be led away to everlasting fire.[4]

St. Cyril, Bishop of Jerusalem (fourth century), declares that the sinner receives an eternal body, that it may burn eternally in fire and never be consumed.[5]

St. Basil (fourth century) pictures the body enduring interminable scourges in the dark and horrible abyss of hell, where there is a quenchless fire and worm punishing deathlessly. There is no liberation from these things, nor any device or means of escaping these bitter prisons.[6]

Hell is never far distant from the thoughts of St. Chrysostom (fourth century), and there is hardly one of his long series of Homilies in which he does not make a more or less lengthy reference to it. Taking them at hazard from the shelf, we find in the Homilies on

[1] Tertullian, p. 217.   [2] P. 193.   [3] P. 194.   [4] P. 199.
[4] P. 206.   [5] P. 208.   [6] P. 213.

Matthew, in the 11th, an admonition of the fearful-
ness and certainty of future punishment; in the 43rd,
" But we have a sea of fire......far greater and fiercer
[than the Red Sea], having waves of fire, of some
strange and horrible fire. A great abyss is there of
most intolerable flame. Since everywhere fire may be
seen moving round like some savage wild beast......
In that place there is burning indeed, but what is
burned is not consumed." Or "Let us pierce our
hearts when we listen to His sayings on hell. For
nothing is more delightful than this discourse." These
sayings, he contends, brace the soul, elevate the
mind, give wings to thought, cast out demons which
so mischievously beset us. In Hom. 4, on *Acts*, we
are told " There is therefore a hell, O man! and God
is good." From Hom. 35, on *Romans*, we learn that
denial of hell is a device of the devil; from Hom. 19,
on the *Epistle to the Ephesians*, that it is our duty to
give thanks to God even for hell itself and the torments
of punishment there; and in Hom. 3, on the *Epistle
to Philemon*, in defending the goodness of God, he
says deliberately " Because He is good, therefore He
has prepared a hell."

In the 20th, 21st, and 22nd Books of *The City of God*
St. Augustine (fourth century) discusses the last judgment and the punishments and rewards after death at
very considerable length. He begins by expressing his
objection to those persons who wrest the Holy Scriptures to quite another purpose, or who oppose them
with fond and frivolous arguments. He proceeds to
quote freely from these same Scriptures to prove that
there is a day of judgment and a resurrection of both
body and soul. He discusses the difficulty raised by
unbelievers as to the possibility of a body enduring
the force of eternal fire, and calls Nature as a witness,
instancing volcanoes, stones, etc. In any case, God's

omnipotency is the ground of all belief in things marvelled at ; " He will do it because He has said He will." He devotes some space to a consideration of the nature of hell's torments : " That hell, that lake of fire and brimstone shall be real, and the fire corporeal, burning both men and devils, the one in flesh, the other in air......Christ has spoken it." Through Adam's sin " came condemnation on all the stock of man, parent and offspring undergoing one curse, from which none can ever be freed, but by the free and gracious mercy of God." Infants must suffer with the rest ; even abortions, if reckoned with the dead, cannot be excluded from resurrection. At the resurrection all shall arise in the stature they were in, or would have been in, in the fullness of man's estate. The body shall be perfect both in quantity and quality ; if its members have been dispersed, the parts shall be restored.

St. Gregory Nazianzen (fourth century) held comparatively liberal views, but his idea of the fate of evil-doers is summed up in the following lines (translated by Dr. Bright) :—

> Whenever I snatch an hour of sleep,
>   Ruthless is night to me ;
> 'Mid searing dreams I lie and weep ;
>   A place of doom I see,
> And forms that stand in chill dismay,
>   Before a Judge whom naught can sway.
> On this side, boiling fierce and high,
>   A fount of quenchless fire ;
> On that, the worm that cannot die
>   Feeds on with gnawings dire ;
> Betwixt, with no indictment scroll,
> Stands conscience to accuse the soul.[1]

St. Jerome (fourth to fifth century) also teaches that

[1] P. 216.

the body of the sinner is incorrupt and shall suffer eternal punishment. Without number or satiety hell swallows those who are punished for ever.[1]

Cyril of Alexandria (fourth to fifth century), of infamous memory, taught that those who die unredeemed continue in great distress and inhabit fire and flames.[2]

Not only did these Christian Fathers insist upon the eternity of hell's torment, but many of them were anxious to make it quite clear that it was torment of the flesh they meant. Tertullian and Chrysostom are both explicit on this point. Augustine held that every man's body, however dispersed, shall be restored perfect at the resurrection. If, asked Jerome, the dead be not raised with flesh and bones, how can the damned after judgment gnash their teeth in hell?

[1] P. 238.   [2] P. 270.

CHAPTER V

VISIONS AND DESCRIPTIONS

Fursey—Drihthelm—Tundale—Owen—Monk of Evesham—
Thurcill—Rolle's *Pricke of Conscience.*

THROUGH the teaching of the theologians, hell
became very real to Christians, and a great number of
visions of purgatory and hell are seriously recorded
by the monks and poets of the Middle Ages. One of the
earliest is the pilgrimage of Furseus, or Fursey, related
by Bede in his *Ecclesiastical History.*[1] Furseus lived in
the seventh century, and was an Irishman of noble
and wealthy family, conspicuous for his piety in his
boyhood, and in course of time becoming a holy man,
remarkable for his singular virtues. At length he fell
ill and seemed at the point of death. In this
condition his soul started on its perilous journey,
conducted by an angel, who showed him the four fires
which will burn the world. The first is for those
who have loved falsehood; the second is for the
avaricious; the third for the stirrers up of strife and
discord; the fourth for the fraudulent and impious.
All these fires met to form one immense flame, which
the angel caused to divide in order to make a clear
path for Furseus. But the unclean spirits were angry
at his intrusion, and hurled one of the damned at him,
striking him upon the shoulder and the jaw and

[1] III, 19.

burning him where he was touched. The holy man luckily escaped without further injury, and was afterwards restored to life and health. But all his life " he bore the mark of the fire which he had felt in his soul visible to all men on his shoulder and jaw ; and the flesh publicly showed in a wonderful manner what the soul had suffered in private."

Another vision reported by Bede[1] is that of the Northumbrian Drihthelm, whose soul was taken to purgatory by a shining angel. He saw a valley, one side of which was filled with dreadful flames, and the other side no less horrid, for violent hail and cold snow were flying in all directions ; both places were full of souls, which were tossed from one side to the other as by a wild storm, and were thus tormented alternately, now by excess of heat and now by cutting cold. He next came to a region of extreme darkness, in which suddenly appeared frequent globes of black flames, rising and falling in a great pit ; these globes were full of human souls, which gave forth an insufferable stench, filling all those dark places. Several fiends rushed at Drihthelm and beset him on all sides, frightening him with their glaring eyes and the stinking fire which proceeded from their mouths and nostrils. His angel, however, rescued him, and, after showing him the ante-chamber to heaven and then heaven itself, he found himself on a sudden once more alive and among men.

Although Fursey was the first, he was by no means the only Irishman to visit the lower regions. Indeed, the place of punishment seems to have had a special attraction for the sons of Erin. Tundale was born at Cashel, and, like Fursey, came of a noble family ; but, unlike Fursey, he was proud, wicked, and cruel,

[1] V, 12.

Fig. 13.—Tundale's Vision

lavishing money on jesters instead of giving it to the Church. One day, sitting at meat in a friend's house, after having given way to a fit of rage, he fell down to all appearance dead, and so remained from Wednesday to Saturday, when he revived and related his experiences. The story of Tundale was for long immensely popular, and the version consulted for this book is taken from the "very nice edition" prepared by W. B. W. D. Turnbull from an MS. in the Advocate's Library, Edinburgh, and published in 1843. The illustration (Fig. 13) is from the engraved frontispiece to this edition. Tundale tells how, attended by his guardian angel, he came to a deep, dark valley, the bottom full of burning coals, on which was a great cauldron, and in it the souls of parricides, fratricides, and other homicides were melted and then strained, as molten wax is strained, through a cloth. Then he saw devils with forks and tongs of glowing iron, tossing wretched souls alternately into fire and cold snow. He saw many dreadful things, and sinners of all kinds : even

> He saw within that dongeon,
> Mony men of relygeon
> That fowle were of fowle venym.
> Both withouttyn and withyn,
> Strong venym in hem he saw
> And on every lym beton and gnaw.

Horrified at all these dreadful sights, Tundale reminds his angel guide of "the word that wryton was"; that God's mercy was everlasting (Psalm c, 5), for here he can see none of it. That "word," replied the angel, "hath deceived many a man"; and he goes on to explain at some length that, although God is merciful, he is also just, and without fear of God's anger the guilty would have no inducement to repent of their sins. So that Tundale might fully realize the

E

extent of God's mercy, the angel shows him more horrors. He saw "a wonder hydous best," that "swollod tho sowlys that wer redy," digested them, and ejected them into a lake where they became souls again. There worms and serpents and other vermin bred in them, and tormented them exceedingly.

> Fro hed to fotte ay was gnawing
> Scrattyng, fretyng, fleying and styngyng
> To hevon the noyse myght have been hurd.

There were the souls of monks, priests, and nuns who had not led holy lives, and so moved was he at seeing them that poor

> Tundale seyd to the angyll bryght,
> Lord this is a dreadfull syght.

But that was by no means the worst. He was taken further and shown a great smithy, where the demon smiths seized him with their tongs and cast him into the midst of the fire, which they blew with bellows until he was molten. Thousands of other souls were fired with him, and when they were molten and glowing red they were treated "as men schull tempore yron and stell"; that is, the molten souls were placed upon an anvil and hammered into one mass. Tundale was at length delivered from this torment by his angel guide, who then promised to show him still greater pains, "sowlys in peyn owttyn ende." He came to a place so cold that "he was ner froson to dedde," and so dark that he was full of fear. He saw more souls burning to ashes, and also Satan, "that lythe bound in helle grond," whom he describes at considerable length. Poor Satan was bound down with red-hot chains on to a sort of large gridiron, and a great multitude of demons blew up the fire under him. Tortured in this way, he roared with fury, he twisted and turned, and in his agony he stretched out his twenty-fingered hands, and, seizing a crowd of souls, crushed them in his hands as a thirsty man would crush grapes to squeeze out the juice. When he groaned souls flew out of his mouth and were scattered far and wide over hell, but as he drew in his breath once more he swallowed them again with pitch and brimstone.

When Tundale had seen all the sights of hell, and seen

> in sorow and stryffe
> Men that wer of wykyd lyffe,

the angel took him to visit the realms of bliss inhabited by those who abide God's will. The details of this visit are outside the scope of this work, and are, moreover, quite unexciting as compared with those of the pilgrimage to hell. When the last word of the story is told, the conscientious editor adds :—

> Be it trwe or be it fals
> Hyt is as the coopy was.

The descent into hell of yet another Irishman, Hoenus, Owen or Owain, in 1153, is related by Henry of Saltrey and Matthew Paris. The legend became very popular, and was soon translated into other languages ; there are at least three early French metrical versions. Owen was a soldier, and had served long in the wars of King Stephen ; having obtained leave to return to his native land, he was suddenly struck with remorse for the life of rapine and violence which he had led. With the licence of his bishop, he determined to do penance at the Purgatory of St. Patrick in Lough Derg, in the hope of finding pardon for his sins. The story of this visit he told to Gilbert, abbot of Louth, who repeated it to many persons ; at last Henry, a Benedictine monk of the abbey of Saltrey, wrote it down. Owen's story differs

E 2

from others of the same character in one important particular—viz., that he visited hell in the flesh, while the others were visits of the soul. As might be expected in his pilgrimage through hell, he was constantly exposed to the assaults of fiends, but invariably escaped by the utterance of the sacred formula :—

Jhesu, as thu arte fulle of myght,
Have mercy on me, synfull knyght !

He saw people of every age and of both sexes nailed to the ground with red-hot nails, and being whipped by devils; men, women, and children boiled in cauldrons; people lying on their backs with fiery dragons, flaming serpents, and toads dining upon their bowels; people hung on iron hooks driven through their feet, hands, eyes, nostrils, ears, or navels over flames of burning sulphur; and so on. From each of these torments Owen himself escaped by calling Jesus to his aid. On leaving hell he passed through Paradise, where he much desired to remain; but, this being forbidden, he found his way back to the entrance of the cave, where he was met by priors and canons, to whom he told his story.

Visions of hell and purgatory seem to have had a horrid fascination for Matthew Paris, for he tells of several. There is, for example, the story of the Monk of Evesham, who on Good Friday, in the year 1196, fell sick, and lay for many days in a comatose condition, during which he had visions of the sufferings of the damned. He saw a wicked goldsmith, who was compelled to everlastingly count out gold coins and swallow them; and other sinners beaten out like metals at a white heat. Some of his descriptions do not bear repetition; they are the outcome of an obscene mind. He compares the multitude of people he saw in hell with a swarm of bees in a hive, and among the damned he recognized many of his own former acquaintances.

Ten years later, in 1206, as Matthew Paris also relates, a simple husbandman named Thurcill, living in a village in Essex, was taken on a visit to the underworld by St. Julian, the "hospitator," who tells him to leave his body in the bed while his soul comes with him. One of the earliest things seen by Thurcill —quite natural in an agriculturist—was a place of punishment for those who had been slow in paying their tithes. In one hell Thurcill saw St. Michael with St. Peter and St. Paul. Here the souls which were perfectly white were handed over to St. Michael, who conveyed them in safety to the mount of joy; those which were spotted black and white fell to St. Peter, by whom they were sent to purgatory; while St. Paul and the devil sat at either end of a large pair of scales, in which were weighed the black souls. When the saint's scale turned down, he sent the soul to purgatory; when the devil's scale was the heavier, he and his attendants threw the soul into a fiery pit. The devils took Thurcill and his attendant saints to see one of their stage-plays, in which a number of punishments were shown. The seats were of red-hot iron, occupied by naked souls chained round the waist, who were seized as required to play a part on the stage. Thurcill, like all the other visionaries, recognized among the damned persons whom he knew. In his story also there are descriptions which may be suited to a monastery, but are quite unfit for lay reading. From hell he visited heaven, saw the blessed and a number of saints, and, after two days and two nights, returned to his body at home; and next day recounted to the priest and his neighbours all the wonders which had been revealed to him.

In the visions of Tundale, Owen, Thurcill, and

others, we find mention of a bridge which the souls have to pass over. This forms no part of the New Testament hell, but it is an important feature in the hells of many of the Eastern religions.

One of the fullest and most remarkable descriptions of the tortures of the damned was written by Richard Rolle (1290–1349), who set up as a hermit at Hampole, about four miles from Doncaster, and who was one of the busiest writers of his day. He wrote religious treatises in Latin and English, versified part of the Book of Job, and produced a poem in Northern English dialect in seven books of nearly 10,000 lines, entitled " The Pricke of Conscience," of which more than a thousand lines are devoted to picturing the tortures of the damned. He begins at the very beginning of man's life, and ends only with his punishment or reward after death.

The dreadfulness of death and the condition of the dying are dwelt upon at some length. Writers usually depict the struggle for the soul of the dying person as between a good spirit and an evil one (as in Fig. 14) ; but Rolle is not content with one evil spirit, he tells how devils gather round the dying man, and torment and frighten him in their efforts to ravish his soul to hell. Good men as well as vile will be tormented on their death-beds. At the resurrection, it is interesting to note, everyone will be thirty-two years and three months old. That ought to simplify the census, if one is taken ; but it is to be feared that it will greatly complicate family relationships.

On Doomsday Christ will judge men in the Vale of Jehoshaphat ; he will sit on a white cloud as doomsman, and will appear austere to the wicked, but very pleasing to the righteous. On the day of doom the earth will quake, the world will burn, and thunder and lightning will strike the wicked. Fifteen accusers will appear against them, of which the first three are Conscience, Sin, and Holy Writ, and the last three Christ's Passion, God, and the Trinity. The picture of the awful day of reckoning is painted in minute detail; but we must not linger over it, except to note that every idle word, every idle thought, and every sin committed through ignorance will be judged, and that Pagans and Jews will go to hell without judgment.

The hermit of Hampole is able to tell us just where hell is; it is in the middle of the earth, and earth is in

Fig. 14.—The soul is seen escaping from the mouth of the dying man, and good and evil spirits are waiting to seize it. (Fourteenth century MS. in British Museum.) From L. Twining's *Symbols and Emblems in Christian Art.*

the middle of the heavens. It may be likened to the core of an apple, or the yolk of an egg when it is hard. The pains of hell are without number, and no wit of man can imagine what they are like; but, fortunately for us, they have been described in books written by "wyse clerkes." With these "wise clerks" for a guide, and aided by his own lively imagination, Rolle goes into details, and explains that there are fourteen general pains suffered by the wicked in hell :—

1. HEAT.—Unquenchable, endless fire.
2. COLD.—So intense that it would freeze a burning mountain.
3. FILTH AND STINK.—

> There sall be mare stynk
> Than tung may telle or hert thynk.

4. HUNGER.—Such that the wicked shall tear their own flesh.
5. THIRST.—Fire, smoke, stench, shall be drink to the sinful; gall of dragons and venom of snakes shall be their wine. There shall be " endeles hungre and endeles threst."
6. DARKNESS.—So thick that men might grasp it.
7. THE SIGHT OF DEVILS.—"The hardyest man in fleshe and bone " would become mad with fear at the sight of a devil; yet the sinful are ever looking upon them ; they see them through the sparks of fire.
8. VERMIN.—Horrible, venomous vermin, which live endlessly in the flames of fire, and gnaw and suck the sinful.

> Vermyn in helle salle be thair clothyng,
> And vermyn salle thare be thair beddyng.

9. BEATING.—Devils strike the sinful with glowing hammers without ceasing.
10. GNAWING OF CONSCIENCE.—The sinful shall ever make lamentation, crying :—

> Allas ! allas ! and walaway !

11. SCALDING TEARS.—More tears are shed in hell than there are drops of water in the sea ; and these tears shall scald and burn, for they are hotter than molten lead or boiling brass.

12. SHAME AND DISGRACE.—The picture of shame and disgrace in hell is not very convincing.

13. BONDS OF FIRE.—The sinful are bound both hand and foot in burning chains; their heads are turned downwards and their feet upwards; by strong pains they are continually strained and racked.

14. DESPAIR.—With no hope in their hearts they shall desire death, but death shall flee from them.

Besides these, there are many other pains not classed in the foregoing list, for in hell there is—

> more sorrow and woe
> Than all the men of earth, old and young,
> Might think with heart or tell with tongue.

There is no peace in hell; the devils keep up a doleful din of roaring and yelling; the wicked are pressed together as in an oven; the damned scratch and tear each other's faces; they are full of hatred and the cursing of their fellows; and yet the sight of another's pain is a fresh pain to them. The least pain in hell is greater than all the pain in the world, and the sorrow of the world is joy compared with the pains of hell.

When Rolle of Hampole describes the bliss of the chosen in heaven, he is particular in pointing out that they will feel no pity there for the sorrows of those in hell, neither for the father nor the son, neither for the mother nor the daughter, neither for the sister nor the brother; none shall have pity for the other.

CHAPTER VI

AFTER THE REFORMATION

Luther — Calvin — Arminius — The Elizabethans — Decker's
Dream—Milton—Pearson's *Creed*—Jeremy Taylor—Christopher Love—Jonathan Edwards—Bunyan.

UNDER the teachings of Luther and Calvin the
pains of hell were insisted upon by the Protestants
and Puritans quite as forcibly as, and even more relent-
lessly than, by the Catholics. The Catholics could
at least buy "indulgences" for their sins, and thus
secure a place in heaven and remission of their fears;
they or their relatives could also pay for masses to
lessen their torments or to deliver them from purgatory. In fact, the fear of hell was made into a
veritable gold mine for the Catholic priesthood of
the Early and Middle Ages; early in the ninth
century Charlemagne complained of the manner in
which the bishops and abbots extorted property from
people by the inducements of heavenly bliss and
threats of eternal torment. The Franciscans and
Dominicans acquired great riches and power by the
traffic in indulgences.[1] The Reformers were inexor-
able and, in this matter at least, incorruptible. "The
human will is like a beast of burden" wrote Martin
Luther in a well-known passage. "If God mounts
it, it wishes and goes as God wills; if Satan mounts
it, it wishes and goes as Satan wills. Nor can it
choose the rider it would prefer, or betake itself to

[1] Alger, p. 418.

64

him ; but it is the riders who contend for its possession." The Augsburg Confession (1530), drawn up
by Melanchthon with the concurrence of Luther,
explicitly requires a belief in the resurrection, in the
universal judgment, in paradise, in hell, and in the
eternity of punishment.

Calvin taught that heaven is attainable only to
those whom it has pleased God arbitrarily to pre-
destine to that end ; all others are irrevocably
damned. " Whence is it," he asked,[1] " that so
many peoples, together with their innocent little
children, should be delivered to death eternal
through the fall of Adam, unless it should please
God?" The Lutherans held that Christ's atonement
brought pardon for those who had faith ; but that
was much too humane a doctrine for the Calvinists ;
they taught that, since God foresaw man's fall and
damnation, only those actually predestined to be
saved would be saved. Both asserted that at the
coming of Christ the dead should be raised bodily,
and after judgment the chosen should rise to eternal
bliss, while the wicked sink to everlasting fire, where,
" Forever harassed with a dreadful tempest, they
shall feel themselves torn asunder by an angry God,
and transfixed, and penetrated by mortal stings,
terrified by the thunderbolts of God and broken by
the weight of His hand, so that to sink into any gulf
would be more tolerable than to stand a moment in
these terrors."[2]

Towards the close of the sixteenth century Jacobus
Arminius, differing somewhat from Calvin as to predestination and free will, nevertheless taught that God
foredooms to damnation all who persist in their
unbelief and withstand divine grace.

[1] Instit. Lib. III, c. 23, § 7.   [2] Calvin.

The Elizabethan dramatists might or might **not** believe in eternal punishment themselves, but they knew that their public did, and consequently we find them using hell's terrors to "point a moral," if they do not exactly "adorn a tale." John Ford (1586–1650) makes Friar Bonaventura describe hell as

> a black and hollow vault,
> Where day is never seen ; there shines no sun,
> But flaming horror of consuming fires,
> A lightless sulphur, choak'd with smoky fogs
> Of an infected darkness ; in this place
> Dwell many thousand thousand sundry sorts
> Of never-dying deaths ; there damned souls
> Roar without pity ; there are gluttons fed
> With toads and adders ; there is burning oil
> Pour'd down the drunkard's throat ; the usurer
> Is forced to sup whole draughts of molten gold ;
> There is the murderer forever stabb'd,
> Yet can he never die ; there lies the wanton
> On racks of burning steel, whilst in his soul
> He feels the torment of his raging lust.

Shakespeare, in *Measure for Measure*, makes Claudio say :—

> Ay, but to die, and go we know not where ;
> To lie in cold obstruction, and to rot ;
> This sensible warm motion to become
> A kneaded clod ; and the delighted spirit
> To bathe in fiery floods, or to reside
> In thrilling region of thick-ribbed ice ;
> To be imprison'd in the viewless winds,
> And blown with restless violence round about
> The pendent world ; or to be worse than worst
> Of those that lawless and incertain thoughts
> Imagine howling !—'tis too horrible !
> The weariest and most loathed worldly life
> That age, ache, penury, and imprisonment
> Can lay on nature, is a paradise
> To what we fear of death.

Thomas Decker (1570–1641) wrote a lengthy poem known as *Decker's Dream*, in which he relates how he "went into the star-chamber of heaven," and was afterwards thrown into a sea infernal, and forced to swim through torrents of unquenchable fire. "Joyes took me in hand in the first dance, but feares and sorrowes whipt me forward in the second." He tells in considerable detail the sights he saw.

John Milton (1608–1674). It is said that the popular notions of hell are largely based upon Dante's *Inferno* and Milton's *Paradise Lost ;* and, indeed, the influence of the latter upon popular faith has been declared to be only comparable with that of Calvin's *Institutes*. Whether this be so or not, most readers of English are familiar with the description in the first book of Milton's great work :—

> A dungeon horrible on all sides round,
> As one great furnace flamed ; yet from those flames,
> No light, but rather darkness visible
> Served only to discover sights of woe,
> Regions of sorrow, doleful shades, where peace
> And rest can never dwell, hope never comes,
> That comes to all ; but torture without end
> Still urges, and a fiery deluge, fed
> With ever-burning sulphur unconsumed.
> Such place eternal justice had prepared
> For those rebellious ; here their prison ordain'd
> In utter darkness, and their portion set
> As far removed from God and light of heaven
> As from the centre thrice to the utmost pole.

John Pearson, Bishop of Chester (1613–1686), published an *Exposition of the Creed*, in which he said : "I do fully and freely assert unto this, as unto a most necessary and infallible truth, that the unjust, after their resurrection and condemnation, shall be tormented for their sins in hell, and shall be so continued in torments for ever, so as neither the justice of God shall ever cease to inflict them, nor the persons of the wicked cease to subsist and suffer them."

Jeremy Taylor, Bishop of Down (1613-1667), whose works have been described as "the most enduring monuments of sacred eloquence in the English language," has a great deal to say about hell in his *Contemplations of the State of Man*. He speaks of the terrible punishments recorded in history or known to experience, but says all these are trifles compared with the sufferings in hell where fathers hate and curse their sons and sons their fathers. In hell the bodies of the damned are so crowded together that they appear as grapes in the wine-press, which are pressed one upon the other until they burst. The eyes of the damned never cease from seeing horrid sights, nor their ears from hearing fearful noises; devils deride, whip, and cruelly torment them without ceasing. The smell is a most pestilential stink, and each body of the damned is more loathsome and unsavoury than a million dead dogs. The wicked shall burn without interruption so long as God is God. The miserable shall suffer a death without death and an end without end; for their death shall ever live, and their end shall never begin. We ought, says the Bishop, to feel "an ardent love and sincere gratitude towards our Creator: that, having deserved hell, he has not yet suffered us to fall into it." Elsewhere he writes: "This temporal fire is but a painted fire in respect of that penetrating and real fire in hell."

Christopher Love (1618, executed for high treason 1651), a zealous Puritan, wrote a series of sermons on *Hell's Terrors*, avowedly for the purpose of startling the conscience of his hearers and readers. He was clearly no great reader himself, for he says that he only knows one English book upon the subject, by a

Mr. Bolton, and very few Latin ones. He divides the subject into a number of queries, of which the first is, "Whether there is a hell?" This he proceeds to answer in the affirmative, quoting the testimony of (*a*) "the heathen" (more especially Virgil) and (*b*) the Scriptures, from which he cites various texts. In his second sermon Christopher Love turns his attention to the query, "What are the torments of the damned in hell?" and says that it makes his heart tremble to speak of what Scripture saith of the torments of the damned; the tongues of men and angels could never unfold the extreme misery of the tormented soul. "If all the land were paper, and all the water in the sea were ink, as many pens as grass upon the ground, as many writers as sand upon the sea-shore, all would be too little to set forth the torments of hell." The gentle Love subdues his trembling heart, and does his best to picture the misery of the damned banished from the presence of God, from Christ's saints and angels, from compassion and from hope. He enumerates the torments under eight heads, which are briefly these :—

1. VARIETY.—There are ten thousand methods of torment.

2. UNIVERSALITY.—All parts of the body and powers of the soul are tormented.

3. EXTREMITY.—He goes into considerable detail upon this point, and says that "the cholick, the gout, the strappado and rack, the burning at the stake; these are but flea-bites to those extreme torments the body and soul must endure in hell."

4. CONTINUANCE.—No intermission of agony. "Says Hierom, the damned in sinning in hell, their sinning is like oil and God's wrath like fire."

5. SOCIETY.—It might be some mitigation of torment if the sinner had good company, but there are only the devils and the damned.

Finally, he tells of (6) the quality of the place, (7) the cruelty of the torments, and (8) the eternity of suffering ; and his descriptions are made all the more nauseous by the "O! beloveds" with which he interlards them.

In his third sermon Love explains that torment in hell must be eternal, because the justice of God can never be satisfied, and approvingly quotes Chrysostom that so long as there is a God so long shall there be a hell.   Not only is there no end to hell, but there is no end to sin ; the wicked after they are dead go on sinning in hell even worse than they did on earth.

In his fifth sermon the kindly Love puts the query, "Shall most men and women be tormented in hell; yea or nay?" And without hesitation he answers yea, the most of men and women that God hath made it shall be their portion and misery to be tormented in hell for evermore. He says that the geographers have divided the world into thirty-one parts, of which nineteen are possessed "at this day" (*i.e.*, seventeenth century) by Turks and Jews, whose unalterable doom it is to be tormented in hell for ever ; seven parts of the world are possessed merely by the heathen, who are in a like parlous condition. Of the remaining five parts, many are Papist, and a Papist living and dying so cannot be saved. The Scriptures, he says, reckon the wicked as grass-hoppers, bees, briars and thorns, as mire and dirt, as stones, as "fishes of no value," and as vessels of wood.

Jonathan Edwards, the elder (1629–1712), president of New Jersey College, devoted much time and thought to this subject. In his sermon on "The

Eternity of Hell's Torments " we recognize the un-
hesitating *dicta* of the expert.   He is firmly opposed
to the idea of the annihilation of the wicked, as well
as to the faint-hearted suggestion that punishment
may not be absolutely eternal.   He undertakes to
show that eternal punishment is not inconsistent with
God's justice, not inconsistent with God's mercy, and,
therefore, not contrary to divine perfection ; divine
perfection requires such punishment, since God must
infinitely hate sin.   By eternal punishment God
vindicates his eternal majesty, glorifies his justice, and
glorifies his grace in the vessels of mercy.   The saints
in heaven will behold the torments of the damned,
and shall then be sensible how great is their salvation.
Every time they look upon the damned it will excite
in them a lively and admiring sense of the grace of
God in making them so to differ.   A view of the
misery of the damned will double the ardour of the
love and gratitude of the saints in heaven.   It will
exalt their happiness for ever.   It will give them a
more lively relish for it.   With eager zest he describes
the "racking tortures" of hell, from which there is
no hope of relief, even when you have worn out the
age of the sun, moon, and stars ; there is no rest day
or night, there is not one minute's ease ; always the
same groans, the same shrieks, and the same doleful
cries.

In the following passage his exulting enthusiasm
for hell is undisguised :—

"The world will be converted into a great lake or
liquid globe of fire, a vast ocean of fire, in which the
wicked shall be overwhelmed, which will always be in
tempest, in which they shall be tost to and fro, having
no rest day or night, vast waves or billows of fire
continually rolling over their heads, of which they
shall for ever be full of a quick sense within and

F

without ; their heads, their eyes, their tongues, their
hands, their feet, their loins, and their vitals shall for
ever be full of a glowing, melting fire, fierce enough
to melt the very rocks and elements ; and, also, they
shall eternally be full of the most quick and lively
sense to feel the torments ; not for one minute, nor
for one day, nor for one age, nor for two ages, nor for
a hundred ages, nor for ten thousands of millions of
ages, one after another, but for ever and ever, without
any end at all, and never, never be delivered."[1]

And in this : "God holds sinners in his hands over
the mouth of hell as so many spiders ; and he is dread-
fully provoked, and he not only hates them, but holds
them in the utmost contempt, and he will trample
them beneath his feet with inexpressible fierceness,
he will crush their blood out, and will make it fly so
that it will sprinkle his garments and stain all his
raiment."[2]

John Bunyan (1628–1688), whose *Pilgrim's Progress* has been held in honour second only to the
Bible in Puritan households, had a great deal to say
about hell. His *Sighs from Hell ; or the Groans of a
Damned Soul*, published in 1658, went through nine
editions in his lifetime, and, although its popularity
has much diminished, it is still in request ; a Dutch
translation was published so recently as 1860. This
treatise is based upon Luke xvi, 19–31, the story of
Dives and Lazarus, which is dealt with in great detail.
Bunyan says that in dying the unregenerate man
"departs from a long sickness to a longer hell ; from
the gripings of death to the everlasting torments of
hell." After dwelling at wearisome length upon the
various torments, such as we are already familiar with,

---

[1] Edwards's *Works*, Vol. VIII, p. 165.
[2] Vol. VII, p. 499.

he desires to impress upon his readers that he has
"only given a short touch of the torments of hell.
Oh, I am set, I am set," he cries, "and am not able
to utter what my mind conceives of the torments of
hell."[1]   He warns them that they are guilty of the
damnation of others, and asks : "How many souls
hath Bonner to answer for, think you ?   And several
filthy, blind priests ? "   How unwilling should they be
to let father, mother, or friends go to heaven without
them.   "O, loth am I to burn and fry in hell whilst
you are singing in heaven !"   In the *World to Come*
Bunyan also goes into a wealth of detail in his
description of the tortures to be expected in the future
life, and the fiends obligingly display specimen cases
for his benefit.   He finds the suffering of sinners a
source of joy to the elect.   "The saints shall rejoice
that we are damned and God is glorified in our destruction."   In his *Last Remains* he mentions that he
is acquainted with one of the " sort of *brutes* (for
they are scarce worth the name of *men*) " who believed
that God and devil, heaven and hell, were mere words
to frighten children with.   Bunyan was so disturbed
by " the brute's " argument that he retired to a wood
intent upon self-destruction.   He was arrested in his
attempt by the voice of his guardian angel, who
conducted him through hell's territories.   There he
saw Lucifer bound upon " a burning throne, his
horrid eyes sparkling with hellish fury, as full of rage
as his strong pains could make him."   Several
novelties are introduced into Bunyan's hell.   He sees,
for example, damned souls holding converse with a
pious Anabaptist.   A lady, who kept no house lest she

[1] This sentence exactly as it stands appears also in *Heaven's
Glory and Hell's Horror*, by John Hart, D.D. (1628), said
(*Delepierre*, p. 145) to be the only book besides the Bible
which Bunyan possessed.

should be taxed, no treasure in her hands lest she
should be robbed, nor let it out without good security
lest she should be cheated, had molten gold poured
down her throat.   A man on a bed of burning steel,
and almost choked with sulphur fumes, explains that
all the diseases of the body suffered at once are but

Fig. 15.—Frontispiece of *World to Come.*

as the biting of a flea to the pungent pains of hell;
and (by special dispensation we suppose) he discoursed
at length upon this head.   Bunyan, after a time, meets
"the brute," who was known on earth as Thomas
Hobbes, of Malmesbury; Hobbes also entertains him

with a lengthy discourse, and explains that the non-luminous flame of hell exceeded ten thousand times in fierceness all ordinary fire.

Dr. Watts (1674–1748), the popular hymn writer, gave expression to his ideas as to the sorrows of departed souls in prose, verse, and picture. The accompanying illustration (Fig. 15), which is reproduced from the frontispiece of his *World to Come*, shows that he did not leave his readers in a moment's doubt as to the cheerful future he anticipated for them. "In the world to come," he says, "every hour shall be filled with cutting sorrows, for there is no season of refreshment, no diversion of mind, no sleeping there." He warns those "who preach that the gates of hell shall one day be opened to sinners," or venture to suggest that "there is a time of release for them," that they "tempt them to give a loose to their vilest inclinations, and all the flagrant and abominable enormities of their own hearts, when they shall be told that these punishments which the Bible calls everlasting shall one day come to an end." For his part, he believes that the fear of the eternal fire which shall never be quenched restrains sinners, and he therefore exhorts his hearers to "proceed to preach the same terror which the blessed Jesus thought not unworthy of his ministry."

The perusal of hymns of this long-popular divine requires some patience on the part of those who have no inclination towards this form of religious art, and No. 44 must suffice as a choice specimen :—

> With holy fear, and humble song,
> The dreadful God our souls adore ;
> Reverence and awe become the tongue
> That speaks the terrors of his power.
>
> Far in the deep where darkness dwells,
> The land of horror and despair,

Justice has built a dreadful hell,
And laid her stores of vengeance there.

Eternal plagues, and heavy chains,
Tormenting racks, and fiery coals,
And darts that inflict immortal pains,
Dy'd in the blood of damned souls.

There Satan the first sinner lies,
And roars and bites his iron bands ;
In vain the rebel strives to rise,
Crush'd with the weight of both thine hands.

There guilty ghosts of Adam's race
Shriek out and howl beneath thy rod ;
Once they could scorn a Saviour's grace,
But they incens'd a dreadful God.

Tremble, my soul, and kiss the Son ;
Sinners, obey the Saviour's call ;
Else your damnation hastens on,
And hell gapes wide to wait your fall.

Joseph Trapp (1679–1747), an English clergyman of small note, contemporary with Dr. Watts, has also left a contribution to the literature on this subject in a quaint but lengthy poem on "The Four Last Things : Death, Judgment, Heaven, and Hell." Early in the opening lines he thus apostrophizes the Atheist :—

But soft—We stand arrested in our course :
Objections here, of mighty weight, and force
Against these suppositious, fancy'd things
The bloated, or the meagre, Atheist brings.
Atheist I stile him ; for he's much the same ;
Tho' chusing Deist's somewhat milder name.
Speak then, dull Infidel, thy inmost thought :
Death's nought, thou sayest, and after death is nought;
A future state, vile Priestcraft's bugbear theme,
And all revealed religion is a dream.
But canst thou prove this ?   No, not tho' 'twere true.

Although it is so wicked of the "dull Infidel" not to be able to prove a negative, the bright and reverend minister of God is in no wise disturbed that his affirmations are equally unprovable, and through pages of halting and turgid verse he descants on death, judgment, and heaven. Reaching hell at length, he opens with this fanfaronade :—

> Tremble, ye guilty ! Tremble ev'n the good !
> Almighty Vengeance ! Chills it not the blood ?

He then pleasantly sets forth the horrors of the infernal regions as follows :—

> Doom'd to live death and never to expire ;
> In floods and whirlwinds of tempestuous fire
> The damn'd shall groan,—fire of all kinds and forms,
> In rain and hail, in hurricanes and storms,
> Liquid and solid, livid, red and pale,
> A flaming mountain here, and there a flaming vale :
> The liquid fire makes seas ; the solid, shores :
> Arch'd o'er with flames, the horrid concave roars.
> In bubbling eddies rolls the fiery tide,
> And sulphurous surges on each other ride.
> The hollow winding vaults, and dens and caves,
> Bellow like furnaces with flaming waves.
> Pillars of flame in spiral volume rise,
> Like fiery snakes, and lick the infernal skies.
> Sulphur, the eternal fuel unconsumed,
> Vomits redounding smoke, thick, unillumed.

Samuel Hopkins (1721–1803), pastor of Newport, Rhode Island, delivered three sermons on " Sin, through Divine Interposition, an Advantage to the Universe," in which he demonstrates, to his own satisfaction at least, that " God's permitting sin was as high an exercise of holiness as any we can think of." No one has ever exulted more shamelessly than Samuel Hopkins in the idea that the torments of the damned will give "ineffable pleasure" to the blessed, and to all who love God.

CHAPTER VII

NINETEENTH CENTURY

Pusey—Newman—Faber—Wilberforce—Spurgeon—God's Indiscriminate Vengeance—Bonar's Hymns—Christian Maxims—The Revolt—Gladstone and Dale—What Unbelief in Hell Means.

THE pronouncements on hell from the pens of certain notable ecclesiastics living within the last fifty or sixty years are scarcely less remarkable than those already cited.

Dr. E. B. Pusey (1800–1882), Regius Professor of Hebrew and Canon of Christ Church, Oxford, was probably unequalled among Church of England divines of his time in his command of descriptive language. The following specimen is from a sermon upon *Everlasting Punishment*, delivered before the University of Oxford on the twenty-first Sunday after Trinity, 1864: "Gather in your mind all which is most loathsome, most revolting, the most treacherous, malicious, coarse, brutal, inventive, fiendish cruelty, unsoftened by any remains of human feeling; conceive the fierce, fiery eyes of hate, spite, and frenzied rage ever fixed on thee, glaring on thee, looking thee through and through with hate, sleepless in their horrible gaze; hear those yells of blasphemous, concentrated hate as they echo through the lurid vaults of hell, everyone hating everyone." Elsewhere[1] he says that "They who deny eternal punishment as

---

[1] *Daniel the Prophet;* Preface.

78

inconsistent with the attributes of God do not really believe in the same God......whom Jesus revealed."

In 1879 Dr. Pusey published a book, which, in a very short time, went through several editions, entitled *What is of Faith as to Everlasting Punishment?* in reply to Dr. Farrar's challenge in his *Eternal Hope.* In his " advertisement," or preface, in speaking of the number lost, Pusey quotes Chrysostom's opinion that among so many tens of thousands in Constantinople at that time you would not find a hundred in a state of salvation. Without actually endorsing this estimate, he is anxious that the possibilities should not be under-rated and the terrors of hell under-estimated. He himself believes " literally " in everlasting fire, and argues that, " If we know anything at all, we know that the doctrine of everlasting punishment was taught by Him who tried to save us from it." He speaks mournfully of Farrar's book as one " of unhappy popularity," and in quoting a common saying, that " the fear of hell peoples heaven," he remarks : " I dare not myself lessen any terror......Perhaps millions have been scared back from sin by the dread of it." He declares that "no one has yet been found to doubt that the mass of Christians have from the first believed the future punishment of the lost to be everlasting," and that " the denial of the doctrine involves the terrible blasphemy that He did not foresee the effect of His own words."[1]

John Henry Newman (1801–1890), first vicar of the Church of England and later cardinal of the Church of Rome, gives a fearful and vivid picture of the Judgment. "Oh, terrible moment for the soul," he exclaims, "when it suddenly finds itself

[1] Pp. 46, 47.

at the judgment-seat of Christ; when the Judge
speaks and consigns it to the jailers till it shall pay
the endless debt which lies against it!......Alas! poor
soul! and while it thus fights with that destiny which
it has brought upon itself and those companions
whom it has chosen, the man's name, perhaps, is
solemnly chanted forth, and his memory decently
cherished, among his friends on earth. Men talk of
him from time to time; they appeal to his authority;
they quote his words; perhaps they even raise a
monument to his name, or write his history." They
speak of his greatness, his great mind, his great
oratorical powers, his excellence, or say that he
was a benefactor to his country and to his kind, but
"Oh, vanity! vanity of vanities! all is vanity! What
profiteth it? What profiteth it? His soul is in hell.
O ye children of men! While thus ye speak his soul
is in the beginning of those torments in which his
body will soon have part, and which will never die!"[1]
If this is the fate of the great, the worthy, and the
benefactor of mankind, how can Christians pretend
that a belief in a future state of rewards and punishments is an incentive to morality? Newman even
pictures the lost soul as having been a Catholic from
a child and dying in communion with the Church;
but even that will not save him from "the flame and
the stench" of his Church's hell!

Father Faber (1814–1863), also a convert to
Roman Catholicism, was the author of a book
entitled *The Creator and the Creature; or, the
Wonders of Divine Love*, which has had considerable popularity, and part of which was republished
as a booklet (*The Easiness of Salvation*) in 1896.
He is one of those curious persons who see "an

[1] Sermon on "Neglect of Divine Calls and Warnings."

awful beauty about the kingdom of eternal chastise-
ment......an austere grandeur about the equity of
God's vindictive wrath." "There is no class of
Christians," he says, "to whom hell is not an
assistance. The conversion of a sinner is never
complete without the fear of hell."[1] Salvation is
so easy: "One confession at the hour of death......
and the soul that has spent close upon a century of
sin is saved, saved because God puts the requisites of
salvation so low."[2] A little later in his book he
asserts that "there may be many in hell who have
committed a less amount of sin than many who are
in heaven, only they would not lay hold of the Cross
of Christ, and do penance and have easy absolution.
There is no life of self-denying virtue, however long
and however laborious, but if it ends in mortal sin
must be continued among the unending pains of hell."[3]

Samuel Wilberforce (1815-1873), Lord Bishop of
Winchester and Prelate of the most noble Order of
the Garter, preaching on "Sin," pictures "something
of the blackness of that darkness, something of the
horrors of that pit, in which ever-new and ever-
overmastered rebellion gnashes in the hopeless agony
of eternal despair," which, he says, is the fate of the
finally impenitent. "Oh! awful sight of unequalled
horror," he cries, "when he who, created by the
loving will of goodness infinite......sees in perfect
retrospect that this his doom of endless misery was
self-chosen, self-inflicted, self-formed in his own
spirit."[4] In a sermon addressed to boys and girls
at their Confirmation, Bishop Wilberforce is even
more definite: "The poet, the statesman, the orator,
the scholar and philosopher, the moralist, the dis-

---

[1] P. 292.   [2] P. 314.   [3] P. 335.
[4] *Sermons between 1845 and 1862*, p. 143.

obedient child, the careless youth, were each in turn described as standing before the judgment-seat, and deceiving themselves still, until the delusion was dispelled for ever by the words which bade them depart into the lake of fire." As a *pièce de resistance*, the young candidates were told of a school-girl cut off at the age of thirteen or fourteen. In her short life she had sometimes played the truant, sometimes told lies, and had been obstinate and disobedient. Consequently she is cut off from heaven and from hope, and henceforward dwells among the worst of men, without any spark of human feeling, without any restraint on their desperate rage. Lost angels are there, in torment themselves, and instruments of others' torture, exulting in the misery of their victims, and perpetually increasing their anguish. "The drunkard they seized and tortured by the instrument of his intemperance; the lustful man by the instrument of his lust; the tyrant by the instrument of his tyranny." This was the teaching of the Bishop to the boys and girls placed in his charge. In another sermon Bishop Wilberforce tells a story of a young man of great promise and of much simplicity of character and excellence of life dying in darkness and despair because he had ventured to doubt whether the sun and moon stood still at Joshua's bidding.[1]

Among the preachers of the nineteenth century few painted hell in more vivid and fearful language than Charles Haddon Spurgeon (1834–1892). He was own spiritual brother (in Dissent) to his Catholic contemporary, Father Furniss. From the earliest years of his ministry to his latest he loved to make play with threats of the wrath of God, and to terrorize

[1] *Life of Bishop Colenso,* by the Rev. Sir G. W. Cox, Vol. I, pp. 160–64.

the faint-hearted into submission. In 1856 he preached a sermon upon " Heaven and Hell " in the open air at Hackney to an audience said to have numbered 12,000 persons. In this sermon, which was republished in New York in 1857, and translated into French and issued at Toulouse in 1858, he drew tragic pictures of the hopelessness of the damned, their anguish and pain ; the mutual recrimination of friends and companions, of mothers and daughters, of fathers and sons. In another discourse delivered about the same time upon " Death : A Sleep "[1] he addresses his hearers thus :—

" If ye were to depart, we might, indeed, take up a very bitter cry : we might ask the owl and the bittern, with their dismal hootings, to assist our lamentations ; we should have need to weep for you, not because your bodies were dead, but because your souls were cast away into unutterable torment. Oh, sirs ! if some of you were to die, it would be your mother's grief, for she would bitterly reflect that you were shrieking and gnashing your teeth in fell despair ; she would recollect that you were beyond the reach of prayer, cast away from all hope and all refuge......O poor soul ! what a sorrowful thing to bid good-bye for ever, one to descend to endless flames, and the other to mount to realms of everlasting bliss." " When the iron gate of hell is once closed on our lost friends, it shall never be unbarred again to give them free exit ; when once shut up within these walls of sweltering flame which girdle the fiery gulf, there is no possibility of flight ; we recollect that they have ' for ever ' stamped upon their chains, ' for ever ' carved in deep lines of despair upon their hearts. It is the hell of hells that everything lasts

[1] Various sermons delivered at New Park Street Chapel, Southwark, 1858.

there for ever......there time never mitigates woe; hell grows more hellish as eternity marches on with its mighty paces. The abyss becomes more dense and fiery! the sufferers grow more ghastly and wretched as years—if there be such variety in that fixed state—roll their everlasting rounds......Then the tortured ghosts are sport for fiends, and the mutual upbraidings and reproaches of fellow-sinners give fresh stings to torment, too dread to be endured."

This well-known passage from his sermon on "The Resurrection of the Dead" would be difficult to surpass for thrill and poignancy :—

"When thou diest, thy soul will be tormented alone : that will be a hell for it ; but at the day of judgment thy body will join thy soul, and then thou wilt have twin hells, thy soul sweating drops of blood, and thy body suffused with agony. In fire exactly like that which we have on earth, thy body will be, asbestos-like, for ever unconsumed, all thy veins roads for the feet of pain to travel on, every nerve a string on which the devil shall forever play his diabolic tune of hell's unutterable lament !"

Spurgeon taught implicit belief in the infallibility of the Scriptures, and in a discourse upon this theme delivered at the Metropolitan Tabernacle in 1888 he warned his hearers emphatically that it was of no avail to argue "God is love, and therefore he will not execute the sentence on the impenitent." "He has not left us inferences, He has spoken plainly and pointedly. He says : 'He that believeth not shall be damned,' and it will be so. If you draw inferences contrary to what He has spoken, you have inferred a lie......Your unbelief in eternal judgment will not alter it, nor save you from it." He had no sympathy with those squeamish Christians who are anxious to cool the fires of hell.

The popular acceptance of the "justice" of the relentless and indiscriminate vengeance of God is vividly expressed by Mrs. Hemans in her *Vespers of Palermo* (Act II, Scene 3) :—

> MONTALBA.   Let th' avenging sword burst forth
> In some free festal hour, and woe to him
> Who first shall spare !
> RAIMOND.   Must innocence and guilt
> Perish alike ?
> MONTALBA.   Who talks of innocence ?
> When hath *their* hand been stayed for innocence ?
> Let them all perish !—Heaven will choose its own.
> Why should *their* children live ?   The earthquake whelms
> Its undistinguished thousands, making graves
> Of peopled cities in its path—and this
> Is Heaven's dread justice—ay, and it is well !
> Why, then, should *we* be tender, when the skies
> Deal thus with man ?

Why should men be tender when Almighty God deals thus with man ?

Horatius Bonar, D.D. (1808–1889), a Scotch Presbyterian divine, was a great hymn-writer and devout servant of God.   He was a prolific writer of religious literature, and nearly every hymnal contains a selection of his hymns.   The following specimen shows that he does not lag far behind that other popular hymnologist, Dr. Watts, in the fervour with which he depicts the condition of the lost :—

> Descend, O sinner, to the woe !
>   Thy day of hope is done ;
> Light shall revisit thee no more ;
> Life, with its sanguine dream, is o'er,
> Love reaches not yon awful shore ;
>   For ever sets thy sun.
>
> Call upon God, he hears no more ;
>   Call upon death, 'tis dead ;

Ask the live lightnings in their flight,
Seek for some sword of hell and night,
The worm that never dies, to smite,
   No weapon strikes its head.

Descend, O sinner, to the gloom !
   Hear the deep judgment knell
Send forth its terror-striking sound
These walls of adamant around,
And filling to its utmost bound
   The woful, woful hell !

Depart, O sinner, to the chain !
   Enter the eternal cell ;
To all that's good, and true, and right,
To all that's fond, and fair, and bright,
To all of holiness and light,
   Bid thou thy last farewell !

Christian Maxims ; or, Tiny Flowers of Ars, is a little book specially prepared for Catholics, and consists of a translation of " selected thoughts " of M. Vianney, Curé d'Ars. The copy before me was published in Dublin in 1887, " permissu superiorum," and had the cordial approval of " C. A. Reynolds, Archbishop of Adelaide." The translator says that these " selected thoughts " have the pith, odour, and essence of Christian perfection, and they may be read and considered with facility, pleasure, and profit. They are certainly rather quaint. Take, for example, one of the selections from IV, on " The Holy Ghost ":—

Take in one hand a sponge saturated with water, and in the other a stone. Press them equally ; nothing will come out of the stone, but out of the sponge you will force water in abundance. The sponge is the soul, filled with the Holy Ghost ; the stone is the heart, cold and flinty, where the Holy Ghost dwelleth not.

From VII, on " The Priest ":—

> After God, the priest is everything.
> Leave a parish twenty years without a priest, and it will worship beasts.

From IX, on "Sin":—

> He who lives in sin assumes the habits and the forms of beasts.

From X, on " Hell":—

> Hell has its source in the goodness of God.
> If you should see a man set up a large pile of wood, and heap up the faggots one upon the other ; and then, asking him why he should do this, he would answer, "I am preparing the fire which must burn me," what would you think? And if you should see the same man approach the flame of the burning pile, and, when it has blazed up, precipitate himself headlong into it......what would you say? In committing sin, that is the very thing we do.
> ......As a bird flies up to the ceiling, and then falls down......the justice of God is the ceiling which attracts the damned.

From XII, on " The Hope of Heaven ":—

> We have two secretaries—the devil, who writes down our bad actions, in order to accuse us ; and our good angel, who writes down our good actions, in order to justify us on the Day of Judgment.
> The devil deserts us until the last moment, as we desert a poor man while the police are coming to arrest him. When the police come, he cries, he struggles ; but they don't let him go, for all that.

These puerilities are actually sent forth to the world under authority, and expressly approved by a Catholic Archbishop, as the " essence of Christian perfection," which it will profit the faithful to read and consider !

G

In the middle of the nineteenth century we see the beginnings of that great open revolt within the Churches against the infamy of an eternal punishment for sinners. Expressions of disapprobation had long been heard in private conversation; but the clergy of all denominations had kept a practically unbroken front towards the public on this and other important, but "hard," sayings of the Founder of their faith. Those who disbelieved in a hell of everlasting torment—and there were many—either pretended belief or else maintained a complete silence. But at last the day came when the silence was broken and the mask of pretence torn off. The dramatic story of the *Essays and Reviews* is admirably told by Mr. A. W. Benn in his great work on *English Rationalism in the Nineteenth Century*. Professor Rowland Williams's contribution, a review of Bunsen's *Biblical Researches*, was specially singled out for condemnation. Under his treatment of the Atonement, "the fires of hell are spiritualized into 'images of distracted remorse'; while heaven becomes 'not so much a place as fulfilment of the love of God.'"[1]   Mr. H. B. Wilson, the moving spirit of the whole production, contributed an essay on "The National Church," and he also was specially selected for attack.   In the course of his argument he urged that "If salvation is determined by belief, either in the Calvinist or the Catholic sense, it is incredible that the conditions of salvation should have been revealed to so few." And finally, "in a passage full of dignity and pathos," he ventured to suggest a hereafter where "all, both great and small, shall find repose or be quickened into higher life." Bishop Wilberforce, whose public allocutions upon hell

[1] Benn, Vol. II, p. 124, *et seq.*

affirmed the fullest belief in its reality and its justice, but whose private opinions are said to have been even more advanced than those of the contributors to the *Essays and Reviews*, castigated the volume in the *Quarterly Review*, preached against it at Oxford, and induced the whole episcopal bench to join in a collective denunciation. Professor Williams and Mr. Wilson were prosecuted for heresy in the Court of Arches, and were suspended from their livings. They then appealed to the Privy Council, where the judgment was reversed by Lord Chancellor Westbury, under whose ruling the eternity of future punishment was declared to be an open question. The Archbishops of Canterbury and York, who sat on the Judicial Committee of the Privy Council, dissented; and Lord Westbury's judgment was so obnoxious to both the High Church and the Low that Dr. Pusey, acting on behalf of both schools, drew up a declaration expressing belief in the verbal inspiration of Scripture and in everlasting torments, which was sent round to every clergyman in England, Wales, and Ireland, accompanied by a letter entreating him to sign it "for the love of God." The declaration obtained 11,000 signatures, which were "won perhaps less by the love of God than by the fear of man."

The prosecution of the *Essays and Reviews*, followed up by Lord Westbury's enlightened judgment, gave a great impetus both to rational thought and to the practice of honesty. As time went on, candid criticisms of the dogmas of the Churches were expressed with a freedom hitherto confined to sceptics, and almost unknown among Christians. In these pages we are solely concerned with the doctrine of eternal punishment, and when Archdeacon Farrar proclaimed his repudiation of this as cruel and horrible he was only expressing the feeling which was widely held by the best minds of his day.   Inside and outside the Churches there was growing up among Christians an increasing perception that eternal punishment was morally indefensible.

The consequence of all this has been that less and less has been said from Protestant pulpits upon the subject of hell.   The silence became so marked and so general that we find on the one hand a zealous Churchman like Gladstone asking what place in the ordinary range of Christian teaching is now found for " the terrors of the Lord," and expressing his fear that there was great danger in this disuse of the instrument of persuasion which St. Paul had thought so necessary ;[1] and, on the other, we have Dr. R. W. Dale, a highly esteemed Congregationalist divine, also commenting upon the general avoidance of the appalling revelations of the New Testament concerning "the wrath to come."   "The appeal to fear," he says, "is being silently dropped......But the menaces of Christ mean something.   The appeal to fear had a considerable place in his preaching ; it cannot be safe, it cannot be right, to suppress it in ours."[2]

The clergy, of course, were, and are, in a great difficulty.   Everlasting punishment is no doubt horribly repugnant to civilized minds, and impossible to reconcile with the idea of a God of love and mercy ; but it is not only explicitly taught in the New Testament—it is absolutely essential to Christianity itself.   This was very plainly put in a

[1] *Studies Subsidiary to the Works of Bishop Butler*, 1896, p. 198.
[2] *The Problem of Immortality*, by Dr. E. Petavel, 1892, **p. 217**, and Supplement No. II.

Lenten sermon preached by the Rev. Dr. Strickland, vicar of St. Saviour's, Hans Place, when he asked: "Is it not a fact that the Fall of Man, the Atonement, the personality of the Holy Ghost, repentance, saving faith, conversion, are denied one after the other by unbelievers in eternal punishment?"[1]

---

[1] *Burning Questions of the Day; or, Plain Truths on Certain Fatal Errors*, 1882, p. 118.

CHAPTER VIII

TO-DAY

Encyclopædia Britannica—Catholic Encyclopædia—G. C. Dewick—"Is There a Hell?"—G. W. E. Russell—Sabbath-Breaking and Eternal Punishment—God Speaking through Disaster.

TO-DAY we find an increasing number of teachers and preachers whose humanity shrinks from consigning even the worst of sinners to an eternity of punishment, and who endeavour to place a new interpretation on the words of Scripture, and to explain away their literal meaning, when they are discussing the question with their equals. For the education of children and for missionary work the words of the Bible are still used without revision, with the approval even of those who no longer accept them as meaning what they say.

In the latest edition of the *Encyclopædia Britannica,* however, hell is still described as a *place*, not a state, as some of the moderns would have it; as the place of departed spirits and the place of torment for the wicked after death. The *Catholic Encyclopædia* (1909) is even more explicit. Rationalists, it is said, may deny the eternity of hell, in spite of the authority of the Church, and professing Christians who are unwilling to admit it may try to explain away Christ's words; but it remains as the divinely-revealed solution of the problem of moral evil. In an article upon "Hell," signed by "Joseph Hontheim," the writer goes fully into the matter. He is quite clear as to the existence of hell as the place where all those who die in mortal sin will be severely punished after death. He remarks that, except by those who deny God and the immortality of the soul, the doctrine has never met with any opposition worthy of mention. He regards it as proved by Holy Writ, the Fathers, the Athanasian Creed (in which the Church professes to have faith); also in the profession of faith in the Second Council of Lyons, and in the decree of union in the Council of Florence, it is laid down that "the souls of those who depart in mortal sin, or only in original sin, go down immediately into hell, to be visited, however, by unequal punishments." The punishment of evil is the natural counterpart of the reward of virtue; it consists in torments of fire, which the greater number of theologians accept as a material fire, a real fire. "*We hold this teaching as absolutely correct and true.*"

The conclusion arrived at by Mr. G. C. Dewick in his Hulsean Prize Essay for 1908, published in 1912, on *Primitive Christian Eschatology*, is that in the span of this life men do not receive their due share of rewards and punishments; the ungodly flourish, the righteous go to the grave in sorrow and suffering. To most people it would be impossible to retain faith in God apart from the belief in the immortality of the human soul and a life beyond the grave......The essence of the doctrine of the resurrection is to maintain that the future life will be more than a bodiless, phantom-like existence......All who believe in God accept the doctrine of a last judgment and retribution in the world to come. Somewhat earlier in his book Mr. Dewick suggests that the objections to eternal punishment frequently arise from moral slackness. To those who love the broad and pleasant paths of easy-going selfishness the stern doctrine of retribution is distasteful.

A notable sign of the times has been the issue this year of a symposium upon the question, " Is there a Hell? "[1] in which fifteen well-known clergymen took part, representing High Church and Low Church, Nonconformist Chapel and Tabernacle, Roman Catholic Church and Jewish Synagogue. All these gentlemen, without exception, gave an unqualified assent to the question put to them. Their difficulties began when they attempted to explain what they meant by hell. Onlookers are proverbially supposed to be moved to compassion at the sight of a " good man struggling with adversity "; but this exhibition of fifteen ministers of religion struggling to persuade themselves that they believe in a hell which is no hell at all is more likely to move to mirth, if not to scorn. The Christian contributors (and it is only with these we are concerned) declare their complete faith in the sayings of Jesus and the most loyal adherence to his teachings ; but each must place his own particular interpretation on those teachings and sayings. They refuse to believe that Jesus meant what he said—or is supposed to have said. When he said " everlasting fire," he did not mean " fire " and he did not mean " everlasting "—he meant something quite different. " Everlasting fire " was just a metaphor, a figure of speech. Other times, other manners ; even for hell. According to these professors of religion, the twentieth-century Christian hell is no longer the place of torment depicted by the poets and theologians of the past eighteen hundred years ; science has quenched its fires and dismantled its chambers of horror ; it is now not even a place at all, but simply

[1] Published July, 1913.

a condition of anguish and remorse, of separation from God, or of enmity to God. While they divest hell of all real meaning, nevertheless these gentlemen cling desperately to the word itself, since without damnation there is no salvation, and the whole structure of Christianity collapses like a pack of cards. Some of them, indeed, like greater men before them, would like to retain the old fear of hell, but the hell they portray is so vague and so unreal that it can neither command respect nor inspire fear. Some try to obscure the issue by referring the derivation of the word to the Saxon *hél-an*—to cover or conceal ; but it is not the *name* of the place of punishment which matters ; whether it is called Hell, Gehenna, Tartarus, Enfer, or Inferno, is of little consequence if we are to understand by it a place of eternal torment for all "whose names are not written in the book of life." Some blame Dante and Milton for the ideas which have been current of the torments of the damned ; but neither Dante nor Milton invented the lake of burning brimstone and fire, the unquenchable fire, the outer darkness where there shall be weeping and gnashing of teeth ; and, as these pages show, lurid descriptions of hell were current in England long before the time of Dante.

Mr. G. W. E. Russell is another Churchman who does not like hell. "Against the theory that God has predestined some of his creatures to eternal misery," he writes,[1] "I will set the Church's faith that God has created all His creatures for eternal happiness, but has left them a free choice to accept or reject the boon. It was a theologian pre-eminent for orthodoxy who wrote : 'Hell is, after all, only the last awful prerogative of the human will'; and it was

[1] "Destiny," *Manchester Guardian*, September 6, 1913.

a Cardinal who said to me : ' I believe in an eternal hell, eternally empty.' " What Christian Church teaches the faith that God created all his creatures for eternal happiness ? Assuredly not the Church of England, through its authorized books ; not the Non-conformist Churches, through their Confessions and Catechisms ; and most certainly not the Roman Catholic Church. As for the Cardinal who could profess belief in an eternally empty hell, he was probably talking idly to amuse himself and his hearers. If he meant what he said, he could not possibly retain his position in his Church and remain an honest man.

That the feeble and ineffectual hell shadowed forth by the clerical contributors to the symposium (to which reference has just been made) is not by any means acceptable to more robust Christians was clearly shown in the correspondence which arose upon it in the daily press. Several correspondents testified their belief to the power of fear as a driving force for Christian missionaries and evangelists, believing with St. Augustine that it very seldom happens that a man comes to believe in Christ except under the influence of terror. Dr. Rouse Ball quoted a recent remark of his ghillie as to a newly appointed minister in the Western Highlands of Scotland, that " a kirk without a hell is no worth a damn." The speaker here humorously expressed a very real state of mind to be found not only in Scotland, but in many other English-speaking parts of the world. It may be further noted, as evidence of how strong a hold the idea of future retribution still has on Pro-testant people, that the Southern Presbytery of the Free Presbyterian Church of Scotland have recently passed a resolution in which they express their sincere grief at

the very painful visitation of Divine Providence at
Cadder coal pit which happened on Sabbath,
August 3, and feel it to be their duty to God and
their fellow-men to protest against the practice of
the Carron Company, inasmuch as it now appears
that they employ their men to work on the Lord's
Day; and also against the action of the men themselves, who deliberately work on the Sabbath in
defiance of the Lord's command to the contrary.
The Presbytery would strongly urge upon employers
and employees, whether in connection with this
company or elsewhere, the great importance of
abstaining from such transgression of God's law, as
Sabbath desecration is a grievous sin which will not
escape punishment in time and in eternity.

If every Sabbath breaker is doomed to suffer eternal
punishment, it is to be feared that the Southern Presbytery will be very lonely in heaven.

In the course of a funeral address at the graveside
of four persons killed in a motor-omnibus accident,
the Vicar of Cheshunt admonished the mourners that
the accident was God speaking, bidding people turn
from their evil ways. There was too much drinking,
too much swearing, too much blasphemy; and through
this warning accident God was testifying his love. The
man who could picture a deity guilty of such a horrible
crime as to upset an omnibus, and kill some of the
passengers, in order to induce some other people
somewhere else to desist from their evil habits, could
have no difficulty in believing in eternal punishment;
his chosen deity is fiendish enough for any atrocity.

We will now turn our attention to three works in
wide circulation at the present time, in which we find
the most lurid teaching concerning sin, the devil, a
material hell, and physical torment. There is no
attempt to palliate any of the horrors here; no faint-

hearted suggestion that hell is a "state" and the devil a figure of speech. The torment is real physical anguish, and the sinner suffers it in his own body. The books to which I refer are the *Mission Pictures*, Father Pinamonti's *Hell Opened to Christians*, and Father Furniss's *Books for Children*.

Chapter IX

" MISSION PICTURES "

In Use from the Sixteenth Century to the Twentieth—The
Soul as "God's Temple or Satan's Workshop."

THESE pictures were originally made and explained
by a certain Michel le Nobel, who was born at
Plongueneau-en-Léon in 1577, and died in the
odour of sanctity at Conquet, at the age of sixty-
five. With certain modifications and adaptations,
these pictures have been in use in France ever
since. That is to say, for full three hundred years
they have been doing their evil work. The illustrations reproduced here are taken from a Breton edition
prepared by the Abbé Balanant, and issued with the
approval of the Bishop of Quimper in 1900, since
when it has been distributed gratuitously and profusely
throughout Brittany. A German edition translated
from the French recently came under my notice; it
was published in Wurzburg at the University Press, and
dedicated to the Bishop of Wurzburg and Bamberg.
From this it was translated into Norwegian, and printed
and published by the Beyers in Bergen; the seventh
edition, now before me, appearing so recently as 1882.
This little book, printed and published by Lutherans
for Lutherans, has for its title *The Mirror of the
Human Heart, with Pictures Showing its Condition and
Quality, either as God's Temple or Satan's Workshop*.
I met with an English version in 1907, in the form of

Fig. 16.—The Soul in a State of Mortal Sin.

Fig. 17.—The Soul Returns to God through Fear of Death and Judgment.

Fig. 18.—The Soul has Seen the Evil of Sin.

a set of lantern-slides, which, with an explanatory lecture entitled " Progress of the Soul towards Perdi- tion," formed part of the ordinary stock of one of the best known lantern-slide makers in London.

The first picture (Fig. 16) depicts the soul in a state of mortal sin, the heart playing the part of the soul, or mirror of the soul. The devil, with hoofs, horns, and bat's wings, occupies the central position in the heart. Above his head are the star of faith and the eye of conscience. Surrounding him are the seven deadly sins: pride (peacock), luxury (goat), greed (pig), sloth (snail), anger (lion), envy (serpent), avarice (toad). Below are the temptations to sin: the mirror, bagpipes, cards, and wine. [It is to be presumed that the bagpipes sometimes induce " profane cursing and swearing," otherwise one wonders why they should have preference over the lute or the zither !] Above on the left the guardian angel is seen praying for the sinner's soul; and the Holy Ghost, in the form of a dove, showers down his favours, which are represented by the "*grenades*," or fireworks, which are flying round the heart.

In the second picture (Fig. 17) the soul, driven by fear of death and the last judgment, returns to God. The monster head, with open mouth vomiting forth flames, represents death, judgment, and hell. The guardian angel, with a death's head in one hand and flaming sword in the other, reminds the soul of the terrors of the under-world. The Holy Ghost approaches close and appeals to conscience, of which the eye is partly closed. Repentance commences, and the powers of grace, penetrating the heart, drive out the monsters and overturn the temptations to sin.

In the third picture (Fig. 18) the Holy Ghost, with his purifying flames, has taken possession of the heart, the seven deadly sins are entirely vanquished, tears are

H

Fig. 19.—The Soul in a State of Grace.

Fig. 20.—The Soul Returns to Sin.

Fig. 21.—The Soul Relapses into Mortal Sin.

in the penitent's eyes, and tears, "still more beautiful," are in her heart. The guardian angel presents a crucifix and a book containing the list of sins committed up to date, and the soul returns to God.

The fourth picture (Fig. 19) shows the soul in a state of grace as a result of contrition, confession, and absolution. It does not look remarkably gay; on the contrary, like the soul in the previous picture, it is distinctly tearful. The crucified Christ occupies the central place, and on either side we see the ladder, the spear, Judas's lantern, and the cock which crew when Peter denied Christ. Below there is a rosary to remind the soul to pray, a fish to suggest the duties of fasting and penitence, a whip for mortification, a church to call to mass, a cross for solitary meditation, an open hand for the bestowal of alms. This last is most important.

The fifth picture (Fig. 20) exhibits a relapse from grace. The sinner has fallen away, so far even as to have her hair curled and to wear a collar of pearls. She is a coquette, and closes one eye upon penitence, keeping her open eye for pleasure. The sins are all coming back; vanity is especially in evidence, and plays a provocative little air in her ear. Below are two lovers pushed towards each other by devils. Love is a dreadful thing; through it sin is once more taking possession of the soul.

The sixth picture (Fig. 21) shows the soul once more in a state of mortal sin. The angel and the dove are driven away, Satan and his servants are in possession. Below we see the "temptations" we saw before, with, in addition, a French novel, some dice, and a mask to show that the sinner concealed his vices. The star of faith has turned black, and the eye of conscience is as though it were dead.

The seventh picture (Fig. 22) is the sinner's death-bed scene. He lies in bed wearing a night-cap, while

Fig. 22.—The Sinner's Deathbed.

Fig. 23.—The Soul Judged and Cast into Hell.

death comes close to strike him with his dart.   At the foot of the bed are the monster head and several devils surrounded by flames ; at the head is the accuser reading the list of the dying man's sins.   His guardian angel turns from the bed, and from above Jesus cries : "Go, thou accursed, to everlasting fire."   About the room are the tools of his wickedness : the pen with which he wrote his editorials for the press, or books, or songs, or other evil things ; a sword, for he killed souls with his writings, his words, and his loose life ; a mask, for he deceived people.   But he will not deceive God ; by him he is judged.

The eighth picture (Fig. 23) depicts the judgment scene and doom.   St. Michael, with the scales (borrowed from the judgment scene of Osiris, and the weighing of the heart against the symbol of truth), the angels with the lists of good and evil deeds, the angel with the flaming sword driving the doomed man away, when he is seized by the devil and carried down into the fires of hell, where he is tormented in all his senses.   Around him are devils, dragons, and all sorts of horrid monsters ; his bed is made of burning coal, his food is flame.

In the ninth picture (Fig. 24) we are shown the broad and easy way to hell and the steep and arduous climb to paradise.   Gentleman and peasant both take the easy road ; one lady has reached the summit of paradise hill, another hesitates half-way, and a peasant has commenced the ascent.   In the foreground there are three women undecided which way to go.   Devils are watching them, but above, they are told, they will find heaven and eternal bliss.

There are three other pictures representing the fate of the righteous, but they are outside the scope of this work.   Besides, they are not very interesting.

Fig 24.—The Two Roads Open to Christians: The Road to
Paradise and the Road to Hell.

Chapter X

"HELL OPENED TO CHRISTIANS"

First Published in 1688—Pinamonti's Predecessor—Holyoake's Reproduction of Woodcuts—Modern Cheap Editions—"Considerations" for Catholics.

A book which has had a long and most astonishing popularity is Father Pinamonti's *Hell Opened to Christians to Caution them from Entering Therein.* Giovanni Pietro Pinamonti (or Pinnamonti, as it is sometimes written) was a seventeenth-century Jesuit, whose *L'Inferno aperto al Christiano perche non v' entri* was first published at Bologna in 1688. It must surely have supplied "a long-felt want"—to adopt an advertising phrase—for before very long (in 1703) a Latin translation was published, an English one in 1715, and a French one in 1857. In addition Spanish, Portuguese, and German translations have also been issued.

Pinamonti's work, however, can hardly be called original, for he had a predecessor in Father Giovanni Battista Manni, also an Italian Jesuit, whose works were very widely circulated on the Continent, although they are very little known here. *The Eternal Prison of Hell for the Hard-hearted Sinner* was issued in Venice in 1667; by 1692 had already reached its eleventh edition; and was translated into German and published at Nurenberg as early as 1677. It was copiously illustrated, and the illustrations in

Fig. 25.—Frontispiece.

Pinamonti's book seem to have been based upon those which adorned Father Manni's.

Pinamonti's *Hell Opened to Christians* was well known to the Freethinkers of fifty years ago, and in 1850 Mr. G. J. Holyoake wrote a pamphlet in denunciation of this work, in which he reproduced the ghastly woodcuts (Fig. 25) with which its author or its editor strove to drive home the lessons of the text. At the present day it is almost unknown to non-Catholics, except by name, and there seems to be an idea that it is no longer in circulation. Mr. Mew, in his remarkable work entitled *Traditional Aspects of Hell*, says that the last English edition was published in 1844; but in that he is mistaken: there are much more recent editions. In any case, I found it advertised in large type in the catalogue of one Catholic bookseller in London, and I bought a copy for a few pence at another Catholic shop without any difficulty.

In his preface Pinamonti tells us that St. Catherine of Sienna wished to place herself in the mouth of hell, and so block up the passage that no more souls might fall into it. Why she did not carry out this laudable desire we are not informed; but Pinamonti, confessing that his fervour was not equal to such a sacrifice, thinks the next best thing that he can do to prevent people "from falling into the abyss of punishment when dead" is to describe its horrors to them. He then proceeds to divide his description into as many parts as there are days in the week. These parts he calls "considerations"; each "consideration" is taken from three points of view, and each has a revolting illustration appropriate to the text.

The first "consideration" is for Sunday's reading, and tells of "the straitness of the prison of hell." The damned are described as being packed together

so closely that they have not even such poor relief
as the prisoner in the gaol may have of pacing up
and down between the four walls of his cell; they
are all heaped one upon another, and bound together
like a faggot. Hell is not only a strait and narrow
prison, but it is extremely dark. There is fire, but
no light; the burning brimstone has a searching
flame which, mingling with the rolling smoke in that
infernal place, raises up a storm of darkness; and the
wretched sinners heaped one upon another help to
make part of that dreadful night. To have not so
much as one friendly ray of light for one day were
horrible, but this darkness is for eternity. Hell is
not only strait and dark, but its horror is intensified
by its terrible stench. Thither all the filth of the
world shall run; and Saint Bonaventura has said that
the bodies of the damned exhale so pestilential a
stench that, if any one of them were to be placed
here on earth, it would infect the whole world, and
every living creature would sicken and die. The
devils also are so pestiferous that their presence may
be readily detected by the unpleasant odour they give
out. Try to imagine, therefore, what the condition
must be when the whole crowd of tormenting, pestiferous devils and all the bodies of the pestilential
tormented are penned up together in this eternally
loathsome abyss.

Having done his best to make Sunday thoroughly
cheerful by his description of the straitness, the darkness, and the stench of hell, Father Pinamonti opens
Monday's "consideration" (Fig. 26) with the text
from Job, " My inner parts have boiled without any
rest," and proceeds to dwell upon the quality of the
fire in hell, its quantity, and its intensity. Our
earthly fire, he tells us, was created for the benefit
of man, but the fire of hell was created "for God to

Fig. 26.—The Fire. "My inner parts have boyled without any rest," *Job* xxx, 27.

revenge himself upon the wicked"; it is a fire in
which the damned shall for ever burn without ever
being consumed. This fire is shut in without any
vent, and the flames as they rise are beaten back, and
return with increased force and unspeakable activity.
This fire in which the damned are burned, without
and within, is so intense that it burns not only the
body, but the soul also; it derives its incredible
vigour from the omnipotence of God, who gives the
flames "such intenseness as he shall think convenient
to revenge the outrages committed against him, and
repair the injuries done to his glory." Imagine it!
injuries done to the glory of Omnipotent God! The
power of the sinner evidently exceeds that of Omnipotence itself.

Tuesday's "consideration" treats of the company of the damned, and opens with the text,
"I was the Brother of Dragons, and Fellow of
Ostriches." For my part I have always felt that to
make a torment out of the company of the damned
was a work of the purest supererogation. I am convinced that if I were being tormented eternally and
intensely, inside and out, in a strait and smelly prison,
dark and fiery, I should not trouble about my
company. I might have archbishops on my right
hand and ostriches on my left, and I should be perfectly indifferent as to who or what might be my
neighbours. Pinamonti and the other geographers and
explorers of hell, however, say that the torment of the
infernal habitation is greatly added to by the ill company found there. We are reminded of the proverb
which says that "it is better to live in a desert land
than with a scolding and angry woman"; and Pinamonti begs us to imagine what it will be like to dwell
eternally with those who are filled with hatred and
desperate rage against each other. He declares that

the fury of a gouty person when he is roughly handled is but a shadow of the despair felt by the wretches in hell whose very groans and howlings make them intolerable to each other. But worse even than the company of our worst enemies will be the company of devils; and the picture of horror reaches its climax when the sinner is told that no devil will torment him so much as the person he formerly disordinately loved. The face which he now thinks heavenly will appear ugly as hell; the eyes which are now his stars will send forth darts more piercing than lightning; the looks he now treasures will be turned into vipers fiercer than any dragon, and at each moment he will reflect for what filth he has lost the beautiful face of God.

After this revolting picture, in which we clearly trace the celibate priest's animus against love, Wednesday's " consideration " is comparatively mild; it dilates upon " the pain of loss." In hell, it would appear, the understanding of man is totally deprived of divine light and turned from the goodness of God; there is eternal enmity and perpetual opposition between God and his creature. For the first time Pinamonti here utters a rational thought. If an Omnipotent God, professedly also a God of love and goodness, treats his creatures in the fiendish fashion depicted in these pages, it is not to be wondered at if the helpless, tormented creatures should feel eternal enmity towards their unrelenting tormentor.

Thursday's " consideration " tells of " the sting of conscience." In the sinner there arises perpetual remorse for his sins; he recalls his past happiness, past power, and past pleasures; he is perpetually driven by racking thoughts; the worm of conscience never sleeps. The damned are tormented by the remembrance not only of the bad things they have done, but by that of the good they failed to do. Thus

Fig. 27.—Eternity of Pain. "My sorrow is made perpetual and my desperate plague refuseth to be cured," *Jer*. xv, 18.

they get it both ways, their sins counting as two for punishment.

Friday's " consideration " is of despair on account of the extension of the pains of hell. A living man is capable of enduring many evils, but not all at one time; one evil corrects another, as one poison sometimes drives out another. But in hell the pains lend each other a fresh sting, and the damned are like so many vessels overflowing with God's anger. In the midst of the curses of detestable companions, in the midst of the blows and insultings of devils, without rest, without comfort, without hope, the sinner is forced every moment to die, as it were, a thousand deaths.

The seventh and last "consideration" (Fig. 27) is for Saturday, and concerns the eternity, the endless-ness of all this useless and wantonly inflicted pain, which is ever increasing in proportion to its duration. " After so small a pleasure, so great a misery," quotes Pinamonti approvingly from St. Bernard ; but it never seems to occur to him that no Deity who had the smallest claim to be described as good could inflict a misery so awful and so prolonged as punishment even for the greatest sin it is in the power of human villainy to commit ; much less could he inflict it for trifling errors, or for the artificial sins so copiously manufactured by the priests. Nor does it appear to occur to the Roman Catholic clergy of the present day that no Church which had the slightest claim to be regarded as a teacher of morality could lend its countenance to such a book of horrors.

CHAPTER XI

FATHER FURNISS'S "BOOKS FOR
CHILDREN"

First Issued 1861—"The Children's Apostle"—St. Alphonsus
Liguori—The "Books for Children" Described—The Teaching Cruel and Immoral.

MOST people have heard of Father Furniss's infamous
production, entitled *The Sight of Hell*, a booklet first
issued in 1861, which is said to have been a great
commercial success, millions of copies having been
sold. But it is not so well known that *The Sight of
Hell* is only one of a series of fourteen penny "Books
for Children" written by Father Furniss, all of which
are obtainable to-day from almost any Catholic bookseller in London. The whole series is lying before
me as I write, and all save one bear upon the cover
the words "Permissu superiorum." The fourteenth
and last, a new and revised edition, has upon an
outside page the "Imprimatur" of "Gulielmus
J. Walsh, Archiepiscopus Dublinensis," the present
Catholic Primate of Ireland. These books, therefore,
are all issued under the direct authority of the
Catholic Church. *The Terrible Judgment and the
Bad Child* and *The Sight of Hell* are perhaps the
most lurid; but all are bad, and utterly unfit to be
placed in the hands of sensitive young people. The
children who pretend to believe them can only be
hypocrites, and those who do really believe them
must live through the days and nights of their lives

in a condition of absolute terror. It is impossible to imagine any teaching that could be more disastrous to childish morality and intellectual sanity.

Father Furniss belonged to an old Catholic family, and was born in Sheffield in 1809. He was the founder of children's missions and of the children's mass, and made a speciality of instructing children in "what every Christian should know," to quote the title of one of his books. His motto was : "Suffer little children to come unto me." It ought to have been : "If little children come unto me, I will make them suffer." He was habitually slovenly, negligent of his appearance, untidy and disorderly, and seems to have had a fine reputation as a liar even among his colleagues in the Church. But godliness ranks before truth, even as it does before cleanliness ; and in 1896, in a letter written to his biographer, the Right Rev. Monsignor Kershaw said that Father Furniss "had evidently been raised up by God's providence to be the children's apostle in these times ; his power over them was altogether extraordinary." Monsignor Kershaw also spoke of "the great good effected by Father Furniss's little books of instruction, of their wide diffusion, the interest they excited among the children, and their general popularity among Catholics on account of their graphic and simple style."

This testimonial from an ecclesiastic of such high standing should be borne in mind in forming an estimate of Father Furniss and his awful teaching. It is, however, only fair to Father Furniss to remember that the horrors he so luridly depicted were not the wholly unaided product of his own depraved imagination, and that he himself seems to have believed in their reality. St. Alphonsus Liguori, the founder of the religious order (the Redemptorists) to which Father Furniss belonged, is among those who have

left descriptions of hell. He spoke of it as a place of
gloom, where light only reveals horror, where the
carcases of the damned lie in heaps unmoved and
immovable, in torrents of fire, which interpenetrate
the brain within the head, the marrow within the
bones, and the bowels within the body. The sight
of sinners will be appalled by the ugliest of demons
dancing upon their prey, their smell by a stench
compared with which all the evil odours of the earth
are jasmine or attar-gul. The souls of the lost toss
to and fro for ever in a fiery deluge like ships upon
an ocean.[1] Whether Father Furniss accepted the
authority of the head of his order as final in this
matter, or whether by dint of constant repetition he
convinced himself of the truth of his own words, I do
not know; but his biographer says that in his last
years, when he was much broken in health, "it
pleased God that he should be sorely tried by
temptation as gold in the furnace. Day and night
he was anguished with many fears, scruples, and
doubts, so as well nigh to despair of his eternal
salvation......It seemed to him as though God's
anger was perpetually threatening him......He would
say that he was lost, and that there was no hope for
him."[2]

There are no illustrations to Father Furniss's
books; they are simply his *talks* to children put
into print. At the period in which the Rev. Father
was "raised up by God's providence" to play the
part of "the children's apostle," lantern-slide illustrations to lectures were not so common as they are
to-day, otherwise we may be certain that he would
not have neglected such a powerful aid. Having no

[1] Mew's *Traditional Aspects of Hell*, p. 309.
[2] Livius, p. 159.

assistance from the artist's pencil, he painted in vivid and sometimes horribly eloquent language the scenes of sin, death, judgment, and hell, with its hopeless, tormented inmates.

The series of the " Books for Children " was issued under the title of *God and His Creatures*, and the first treats of *Almighty God*. It does not, as one might expect, depict God to the children as a God of love; nothing so amiable. It opens with the story of a mission supposed to have been held by St. Francis in Naples. The saint was evidently a man of leisure, and Naples was not the Naples we know to-day—a city with over 500,000 inhabitants—for before the mission began St. Francis went the round of the streets knocking at each door as he passed; and when the door was opened he said: " Please, for the love of God, to come to the mission." At a certain house there lived a very wicked woman named Catherine, who met the saint's request with a blunt refusal; " No, I will not come to the mission," she said. St. Francis called again the next night, but was told that the wicked Catherine was dead. St. Francis went to the body, and in a loud voice commanded Catherine, in the name of God, to say where her soul was. The body opened its mouth, and the dead tongue moved inside the head, and said in a frightful voice, "*I am in hell.*" "You see," comments Father Furniss, " how angry God is when people do not go to a mission or a retreat when they can." Catherine is spoken of as a very wicked woman, but no particular offence is charged upon her except that she refused to go to the mission; for that refusal Almighty God murdered her and sent her soul to hell. What a lesson in loving-kindness for little children !

After stories of St. Anthony and the fishes, and the

repentance of Thais, and injunctions to remember that God is present with the child everywhere and always, we have a sure and certain recipe for cheating the devil. The devil says to himself: "There's a child about to pray; let me tempt it"; and he sets off instanter on his errand of evil. But when he gets there he is too late; the prayer is finished. This illustrates the value of the frequent repetition of short ejaculatory prayers — the sort of thing Cardinal Vaughan was so fond of[1]—because if the prayer is finished by the time the devil arrives he has no power to distract the mind. Then we have a succession of stories to show how easily God made the world, how all things obey God, and how God loves his creatures. In order to meet the difficulty of the blind, the deaf, the lame, and the lunatic, Father Furniss assures the children that these seeming misfortunes are really the greatest blessings. Nothing comes by accident; all is fixed by God.

The second book, *God Loves Little Children*, is largely composed of anecdotes of the wonderful childhood of the saints and other holy men and women. Sometimes Father Furniss treads on rather dangerous ground, as, for example, when he tells of St. Rose, who did not like the trouble of learning to read and write. She was scolded by both mother and priest; and the next day, in saying her prayers, she asked God to teach her. Marvellous to relate, when she went to her mother she found she could now read and write—"God himself had taught her when she was praying." If backward boys and girls try St. Rose's royal road to learning, their certain disappointment may possibly lead them to unbelief. This book concludes with a "rule of life" for

[1] *Cardinal Vaughan*, by J. G. Snead Cox, p. 450.

children, which is mainly made up of prayer. The "daily virtues," of which very few are enumerated, are all to be done for Jesus; without this there is no salvation. The "good practices" consist, without exception, of religious ceremonies. Parents are reminded of the immense importance of the prayers of children, for it was "the prayers of little children which saved the Church of God in the midst of persecution."

The fourth book is called *The Great Evil*, and depicts the awfulness of mortal sin. With callous unconcern Father Furniss tells how a child was deliberately and cruelly left alone in the dark with a dead body, and how it was so terribly frightened that it died. He then proceeds to tell sinful little children that they have within them a "frightful hideous monster of a dead soul," more fearful by far than the dead body which frightened the child to death. He describes in detail a body broken in all its limbs, and disfigured inside and out by "every disease in the world"—he fairly revels in minute and loathsome descriptions of the decomposing body in the grave—but "O sinner, your soul is ten million times worse." In a later attempt to paralyse the child's mind by terror, this Redemptorist Father tells him that when a child commits mortal sin his soul is thrown into a den of devils, "a million times more cruel and frightful than lions and tigers and serpents and adders and scorpions and toads and spiders." It is rather quaint to find "toads and spiders" coupled with "lions and tigers," but they would be much more familiar, and consequently much more offensive to little children, especially to little girls, than the other wild beasts. The devil is likened to the boa-constrictor, which winds itself round and round a man "as you might wind some thread round a stick till nothing of the stick could be seen......It crushes the head and the arms and all the body till it has crushed all the blood out of the flesh and the soul out of the body. Then he eats up all the crushed flesh......Then the serpent lifts up his great, fierce, cruel head, and opens his terrible mouth, and shoots out a tongue made of fire, and hisses at your soul, and bites it with his fiery tongue......This sting of the devil is called the *Sting of Death.*" The only way in which mortal sin may be forgiven is by confession, followed by absolution and the sacrament of penance.

In the sixth book, *For Young Persons*, the theatre is spoken of as " the devil's house." And the devil is so astute that he gets cheap theatres—twopenny, and even penny, theatres—for those who cannot afford to pay much. Father Furniss rates the devil's powers so highly, and has so little confidence in the goodness of his Almighty God, that he is of opinion that there is scarcely any employment for the young in which there is not some particular occasion for sin. He specially mentions those who carry baskets, oranges, apples, grit, sand, and pipe-clay as being in need of a great grace from God to save their souls. His corrupt mind sees immorality rampant everywhere; those who go to lonesome places, or to markets or fairs, or on errands, are all in danger; letter writing is very risky, and emigration provides the worst possible temptation. Young men and young women who are engaged should never be alone together, nor take long walks, nor even indulge in long conversations. If they want to speak to each other, it should be in the presence of their parents or some well-conducted person. It is amazing that the morality of any young people could survive such evilly suggestive teaching as this.

If we are to believe Father Furniss, nothing is easier

to a child than to go to hell ; the difficulty for him is to keep out of it. How difficult we learn from the ninth and tenth books of his series " for children and young people." Death itself is made a thing of horror ; the child is told that it is fearful to watch a human being going out of the world. The dying person is represented as frequently showing signs of fright ; even holy persons and saints are terrified at the thought of coming before the judgment-seat of the Lord Jesus Christ ; and if holy men die in such agonies of fear, what must be the case with ordinary mortals ?

Having worked up the minds of his youthful disciples to a satisfactory condition of fear, Father Furniss proceeds to relate the shocking story of the fate which befalls the bad child, a poor little unfortunate to whom we are introduced at the very moment of death. Immediately in that first quiet moment after death, the child stands before the judgment-seat of Jesus Christ. The heavens open, and millions and millions of angels and archangels come forth ; but deep down below the gates of hell open also, and devils pour forth like a black torrent ; flashes of fire come from their eyes, and the air is darkened by their frightful forms. The angels go to the right of the judgment-seat, and the devils to the left. The angel guardian of the child comes forward, and, standing at the child's right hand, holds the book in which are written all the child's good works ; a devil, the accuser, goes to the child's left hand, and holds the record of his sins. The devil opens the proceedings by reading the list of sins, and is followed by the angel guardian with the list of good works. These are enumerated by Father Furniss, and it is noticeable that until we come quite to the bottom of the list, with a cursory mention of good works to the poor, obedience to parents and kindness to companions, the whole of the "good works" named are connected with religious observances of one kind or another, just as a large proportion of the sins consist of the omission of religious observances. When the angel guardian has finished, the devil asks leave to say another word, and then proceeds to claim that many of the good works enumerated by the angel are invalid, since they were not done in the name of the Lord Jesus Christ; his claim is allowed, for "*all the good works not done for Jesus are counted for nothing.*"

Things look pretty bad for the poor child; but there is a ray of hope, for it appears that all this accusation and defence, and further accusation, is mere preliminary talk, and settles nothing. The child's future state does not depend upon its record of good or bad deeds; it depends upon one single thing—viz., whether at the moment of death there was or was not a mortal sin in its soul. It might have been doing good deeds all its life, and at the moment of death committed its one and only sin; and this sin, being unrepented and unconfessed, would counterbalance the whole of a well-spent life. Jesus commands that the state of the child's soul should be made clear; and then—"Oh, the frightful, the terrible, the horrible sight—*there is mortal sin there!*" The angels turn away in horror, and Jesus looks at the wicked child in anger. The child pleads piteously; it was so little, so weak, so ignorant, so tempted. But Jesus has no mercy; he admits no plea. At last, its heart bursting with sorrow and anguish, withering with fear and dread, the child ceases its prayers.

A deep and terrible silence ensues, and Jesus passes sentence :—

You shall never, never see my face any more. You have chosen during your lifetime to obey the devil rather than to obey me. Therefore, with the devil you shall be tormented in hell. The smoke of your torments shall rise up before me night and day. Your painful cries shall come to me for ever and ever. But I will never listen to them.

Jesus then proceeds to curse this "wicked" child in the name of God the Father Almighty, who made him, in the name of himself (God the Son), and in the name of the Holy Ghost; and, more frightful than all the lightnings of the world, the flames of the curse strike the child through and through. He sees devils, thousands and millions of them, coming at him more swiftly than the wind, as hungry dogs would come at a bone. His cries of anguish are drowned in the uproar of their blasphemies. The gates of hell are opened, and his brain gets wild and mad with fright. There is no mercy in "God the Father Almighty, who made him," none in the tyrant God the Son; the child is thrown into hell, the gates are shut, and day in and day out for all time this pitiful little sinner is pictured as burning in hell. "Suffer little children to come unto me, for theirs is the kingdom of hell," says Father Furniss's Jesus.

So that every child may fully understand the fate that awaits him, Father Furniss gives a detailed description of hell and its torments. The prison of hell, he thinks, is in the middle of the earth, and therefore about four thousand miles from where we stand. The gates of hell, he tells the children, are of vast thickness and tremendous strength—as they had need to be, for there are millions and millions of sinners shut up in hell, and this multitude, strong in their fury and despair, are continually dashing themselves against these massive gates. Do you hear that growling thunder rolling from one end of hell to the other? The gates of hell are opening. Look within, and you see the floor like red-hot iron, with streams of burning pitch and sulphur running through it. The floor blazes up to the roof, and hell is filled with a fog of fire, while torrents of fire and brimstone rain down. Take a little spark of kitchen fire, throw it into the sea, and it will go out. Take a spark from hell, less than a pinhead, throw it into the ocean ; it will not go out. In one moment it would dry up all the waters of the ocean, and set the whole world in a blaze.

Fire on earth gives light ; the unquenchable fire of hell is *dark*, thick, black, heavy aching darkness ; darkness made worse by the smoke, great sulphurous clouds for ever rising and for ever beaten back again. And the *noise*. You may have heard the last shriek of a drowning man ; you may have heard the wild cry of the madman, the roar of the lion, or the hissing of the serpent ; but all that is as nothing to the screams of fear, the cries of agony, and the shrieks of despair of the millions and millions and millions of tormented creatures in hell. Above these cries, above the gnashing of teeth and the blasphemies of devils, you hear the roaring of the thunders of God's anger, which shakes hell itself to its foundations. But there is still another sound, an awful sound—the sound of the tears running night and day from countless millions of eyes, plashing, plashing down on to the burning floor of hell. Father Furniss next tells of the dreadful, sickening smell in hell, quoting Joel ii : "*His stench shall ascend, and his rottenness shall go up*"—and, of course, Saint Bonaventura.

After this there is a lurid description of great Satan bound with red-hot chains, who, himself a prisoner, is yet the judge of the damned, whom he sentences to the torments he considers appropriate to their offence.

Now, says Father Furniss to his audience of "children and young persons," it is time to see where the sinner has been put. He shows the sinner lying for hundreds of millions of years on the same side on a scorching, broiling bed of fire; all the body is *salted with fire*. Then there are the sinners who are eternally eaten by worms and insects, who make a dwelling-place in the mouth and ears and eyes; who bite and sting through all eternity. Or there is the torment of fright. Little boys have been known to die of fright, or to be driven out of their senses; but their fright is a small matter compared with that which the sinful child will feel in hell. This awful priest, whom the Right Rev. Monsignor Kershaw declared "had evidently been raised up by God's providence to be the children's apostle," next throws open the doors of some of "the dungeons of hell." In the first he shows a girl wearing

> a bonnet of fire. It is pressed down close over her head; it burns into the skin; it scorches the bone of the skull and makes it smoke......Think what a head-ache that girl must have......She is wrapped in flames, for her frock is on fire......There she stands burning and scorched; there she will stand for ever burning and scorched!......When that girl was alive......she cared only for one thing, and that was dress!...... And now her dress is her punishment.

In another dungeon is another girl standing with bare feet on a red-hot floor:—

> The door of the room has never been opened before since first she set her foot on that red-hot floor. Now she sees the door opening. She rushes forward......"Look," she says, "at my burnt and bleeding feet. Let me go off this floor for one moment, only for one single short moment. Oh, that in this endless eternity of years I might forget the pain only for one single moment......" Oh, that

you could hear the horrible, the fearful scream of that girl when she saw the door shutting never to be opened any more. The history of this girl is short. Her feet first led her into sin, so it is her feet which most of all are tormented.

In the fourth dungeon is a boy :—

His eyes are burning like two burning coals. Two long flames come out of his ears......Sometimes he opens his mouth, and breath of blazing fire rolls out. But listen ! there is a sound just like that of a kettle boiling. Is it really a kettle boiling ? No ; then what is it ? Hear what it is. The blood is boiling in the scalding veins of that boy. The brain is boiling and bubbling in his head. The marrow is boiling in his bones. Ask him why he is thus tormented. His answer is that when he was alive his blood boiled to do very wicked things.

In the fifth dungeon is the little child whom we saw before the judgment-seat of the Lord Jesus Christ :—

The little child is in this red-hot oven. Hear how it screams to come out. See how it turns and twists itself about in the fire. It beats its head against the roof of the oven. It stamps its little feet on the floor. You can see on the face of this little child what you see on the faces of all in hell—despair, desperate and horrible !......*God was very good to this child.* Very likely God saw that this child would get worse and worse, and would never repent, and so it would have to be punished much more in hell. So God *in His mercy* called it out of the world in its early childhood.

Can anyone—any grown person—read these descriptions without feeling a very sickness of horror ? What, then, must be their effect upon the impressionable minds of sensitive little children ? We have laws specially designed, and still enforced, to prevent men from expressing their honest disbelief in the Christian religion ; but there is no law to prevent men with perverted minds from using this same religion to torture young children and corrupt their morals by the narration of ghastly horrors such as these. The law says, Christian public opinion says : Be honest and upright in the avowal of your disbelief, and we will punish you by prison and social ostracism ; but profess belief, and in the name of your belief invent lie upon lie to work upon the innocence and credulity of the little ones, and you shall be hailed as an ornament of society and a benefactor of mankind ! Some Freethought speakers are sometimes reproached with being coarse ; could there be anything more really coarse than the impure suggestions found in Father Furniss's *Books for Children ?* Some are reproached with being offensive ; by no possibility could any Freethought speaker be so horribly offensive as this Yorkshire priest. They are reproached— nay, they are imprisoned, for advocating opinions tending to the dishonour of Almighty God ; but no words of theirs could possibly dishonour the Christian Deity so much as this representation of him as an Almighty Fiend, exulting in cruelty, without one spark of mercy or compassion.

CHAPTER XII

CONCLUSION

Hell and the Higher Civilization—Effect of Belief upon Character—Fear as an Incentive to Morality—The Fear of Death—The Leaven of Doubt—Educated Protestants and the New Hell—No Heaven without Hell—Schools, Missions, and Masses—The Struggle for Intellectual Freedom.

THE doctrine that the condition after death is definitely awarded as compensation or retribution for conduct in this life—or, more shortly, the doctrine of retribution—forms no part of the early beliefs in a future life. Hence it is claimed as an ethical doctrine belonging to a higher civilization. While it is quite true that the belief in a hell of punishment is found only in what is usually styled a "higher" civilization, nevertheless it is in no way an essential part of the higher development of mankind. There are various painful diseases and evil practices unknown to primitive peoples, and found only in a higher civilization; but they are no essential part of it, and civilization has everything to gain by their removal. Similarly, the belief in hell may be looked upon as a morbid growth, a disease, and no true part of the bone and sinew of a healthy and advancing civilization. Because the doctrine is found only in the later stages of the evolution of man, to conclude that it is a necessary or desirable part of it is to ignore the fact that there have been, and are, highly civilized individuals and peoples absolutely devoid of any such belief. To claim it **as** an "ethical" doctrine is to cast a slur upon ethics.

What effect has this belief in the torments of hell— the "most terrific superstition that has ever weighed upon the human mind"—had upon the character and conduct of men? Has it made them happier, more moral? Dr. E. B. Tylor, whose splendid services to the history of mankind cannot be over-estimated, thinks it plain that "the doctrine of future judgment has been made to further goodness and check wickedness, according to the shifting rules by which men have divided right from wrong."[1] I have already, early in this work, referred to Herbert Spencer's opinion that the anticipation of future torments or future joys is necessary to the great mass of men. One hesitates to dissent from such authorities, but is it really true that a belief in hell has furthered goodness and checked wickedness? is it true that few are wholly fitted to dispense with this belief? Profound erudition or exceptional ability is not required to form an opinion on this point; all that is necessary is a little common sense and some acquaintance with facts of history. Spencer says "the effects of a belief upon conduct must be diminished in proportion as the vividness with which it is realized becomes less," and, assuming that to be so, we may inquire whether the belief in eternal punishment, even when most vividly realized, has ever had much effect upon conduct? It has made good men miserable, but it has never made bad men moral. The Golden Age of the Christian religion in Europe was the Dark Age of civilization. Everywhere the lowest standard of morals has been current where belief in hell has been most vivid. Lecky tells us that the seventh and

---

[1] *Primitive Culture*, 1873 ed.; Vol. II, p. 106.

eighth centuries formed the darkest period of the
Dark Age—every kind of vice was rampant, virtue
was rare. Yet this was an eminently religious period—
all literature was sacred, and there was little or no
heresy; priests and monks acquired enormous power
and wealth, kings abandoned their thrones for the
cloister, and saints appeared by the hundred.[1] If we
come down to a period nearly a thousand years later,
and look close at home, we see the miserably servile
condition of the Scotch people and their harshness and
moroseness of character under the intimidation of
their clergy, who uttered the most appalling threats of
future punishment for the most trivial "sins." The
people believed that in this world they were incessantly
pursued by the devil, while in the next the most frightful punishments awaited them. Under this blighting
doctrine men became soured, troubled, and downcast;
the fairest and most endearing parts of their nature,
being constantly repressed, almost ceased to bear
fruit. The unsocial, cruel doctrines of their faith
destroyed not only human pleasures, but human
affections also; they ruthlessly broke domestic ties
and encouraged the vilest form of selfishness, by
teaching each individual to concentrate his whole
attention on the salvation of his soul.[2] It is, indeed,
freely admitted that, when belief in hell was most
vividly realized, "the conception of a spiritual destiny
was made to justify the most ghastly crimes. Man
was preordained to do certain acts, and when he did
them he was merely obeying an irresistible decree,
and was in no sense amenable to moral censure."[3]

[1] *History of European Morals*, R.P.A. ed.; Vol. II, pp. 90–102.
[2] *Buckle's History of Civilization*, Vol. III, chap. iv.
[3] G. W. E. Russell on "Destiny."

K 2

This "ethical" doctrine of retribution, which is the foundation-stone of the Christian religion, lighted the fires of the Inquisition, furnished the rack and the torture chamber, and dehumanized men everywhere. For a brief but comprehensive exhibition of the "general violence, grossness, cruelty, and licence" which characterized the ages of faith, the student cannot do better than consult Cotter Morison's *Service of Man*. This able and learned writer shows that "not in one country, nor in one age, but all through the ages of faith, the most flagrant breaches of the moral law are quite compatible with the most fervent and complete belief in God, in the Bible, and, in short, in Christianity." Assent to Christian dogmas offers no guarantee for good conduct. " There never was a moment, from the first teaching of Christianity to the present day, when sincere pastors have not deplored the condition of the greater part of their flocks. That the whole world lieth in wickedness is the constant burden of their complaint. Could better proof be required or given that the supposed connection between belief and morals is illusory ? "

So far, indeed, from inculcating ethics, the doctrine of future retribution has been the inspiration of excesses of the most horrible character. Constant dwelling upon the searing descriptions of the awful torments inflicted by a so-called just and loving Deity for the most trifling errors, blunted human sensitiveness, and made men intolerant and brutal where, moved by reason, they should have been tolerant and kind. Just as there was no proportion between "crimes" and the punishments ordained for them by Almighty God, so the zealous Christian observed no proportion in his punishments. The anguish of the tortured heretic, the blood of the innocent dissident—massacred singly, by the score, and by the thousand—will for ever cry out and bear witness against the "ethics" of this man-hating creed. Humaner ideas in the treatment of the sick, in the punishment of the criminal, in the usage of the enemy, in the sufferance of the heretic, have only been growing up with the decline in a realized belief in hell.

In isolated cases, here and there, it may be that the fear of hell has been, as Burns says, "the hangman's whip" which has kept the wretch in order, but it certainly has never moralized mankind. Even in these isolated cases it is doubtful whether the result has not been due quite as much to the fear of man as to the love of God. The attempt to make men moral by the threat of future punishment is an attempt to intimidate into morality, to coerce by fear. The ethics of mankind should be built upon the rock of reason, not upon the shifting sands of cowardice. The ultimate result of intimidation, whether in politics, religion, or social matters, is that the strong, the brave, and the reckless will to a greater or less extent disregard any threats which stand in the way of what they think right or what they desire. It is only the feeble who can be disciplined by the rod in the cupboard; and even they, in their hour of passion, are apt to find a temporary courage which enables them to disregard all risks. Intimidation may also restrain for a time men of low intelligence, but it has no permanent value. Morality bred of fear is a poor sort of thing, liable to break down directly the fear of future punishment is outweighed by present cupidity, or any other strong passion. Moreover, what morality could be expected to result from a creed which teaches that belief is everything, conduct nothing? which teaches that the virtuous may be in hell and the wicked in heaven, because so long as a sinner repents, even after "close upon a century of sin," and is absolved, his salvation is assured ; while a life of self-denying virtue will not win heaven without the Cross of Christ.[1]   " Joy shall be in heaven over one sinner that repenteth more than over ninety and nine just persons which need no repentance."[2]

Nothing is more strenuously insisted upon in the New Testament than the blessings of poverty and the future punishment of the rich; but, save in a very few cases, the fear of hell has never prevented Christians from accumulating wealth.   The greatest and most terrific torments of hell are in every religion reserved for the unbeliever, yet there has never been a period nor a religion without its unbelievers.   It is not the fear of tortures beyond the grave which has impeded the tendency to unorthodoxy, but the persecution of man ; and even this could only delay, it could not finally prevent, divergence from accepted creeds.

The uncertainty of the future life, the dread of eternal damnation, the thought of the impending struggle with the devil for the possession of his soul, of the last judgment, of the awful Judge—all this has made death itself a fearful thing to the believing Christian.   " It were a light and easy matter," said Martin Luther, " for a Christian to suffer and over- come death if he knew not that it were God's wrath ; the same title maketh death bitter to us.   But an heathen dieth securely away ; he neither seeth nor feeleth that it is God's wrath, but meaneth that it is the end of nature, and is natural."[3]   The feeling of despairing envy so poignantly expressed by Bunyan when he said, " I blessed the condition of the dog and toad, because they had no soul to perish under

---

[1] See p. 81.   [2] Luke xv, 7.
[3] Lecky's *Rise of Rationalism*, Vol. I, p. 137.

the everlasting weight of hell!"[1] must have been the experience of countless Christians. Compared with this, the state of the dying unbeliever is happy indeed ; to him death brings no such bitter fear, no such shrinking horror ; the future holds for him neither a "barbaric heaven nor a monstrous hell";[2] he neither hopes nor fears. Life may be quitted with sorrow and passionate regret, but the portals of death open for him upon a deep and dreamless sleep.

> This little life is all we must endure,
> The grave's most holy peace is ever sure,
>   We fall asleep and never wake again ;
> Nothing is of us but the mouldering flesh,
> Whose elements dissolve and merge afresh
>   In earth, air, water, plants, and other men.[3]

As we look at pictures such as those reproduced in these pages, and read the terrible language used by representative Christian teachers during nineteen centuries of Christianity in consigning innocent "sinners" to eternal torments, and study the awful descriptions of these torments, we may get some idea of the disastrous effect this teaching must have had upon the people who really believed in it. We may wonder that they did not all go mad with fear. There must surely always have been a leaven of doubt, otherwise men could not have preserved their sanity. It is this leaven of doubt, which up to a hundred years ago was so small and so weak, and which in some minds to-day is still so small and weak, that we need to see grow and strengthen, until it entirely expels this corroding superstition, this immoral doctrine of eternal torment.

Among educated Christians this leaven of doubt

[1] Alger, p. 661.
[2] Maeterlinck, *Fortnightly Review*, September, 1913.
[3] *The City of Dreadful Night*, by "B. V.," p. 37.

has already taken firm root, both in the minds of the sheep who are gathered into the ecclesiastical fold, and in the minds of the shepherds who herd the flock. Among educated Christians—Protestant Christians at least—the best minds are ashamed of hell to-day. They profess to accept the teaching of Jesus, but they must put their own interpretation upon what he is supposed to have said. By the aid of their new interpretations they have constructed a new hell which has nothing in common with the old except the name. It took the Church ten centuries to reject a hell of torment for unbaptized infants and construct a painless *limbus* for them ; and it has taken nearly another ten centuries to reject a hell of torment for adults and construct for them a *limbus* free from physical pain. There is no doubt that the more enlightened and far-sighted among the clergy would be glad to dispense altogether with this immoral dogma of hell ; there must be many to-day who realize the truth of what F. W. Newman said fifty years ago, that " the weight of hell will totally sink Christianity if it is not cut away "; but they are faced with the difficulty that heaven and hell stand or fall together. If you cut away hell, heaven goes also. In the recent symposium referred to in a previous chapter, it was generally agreed that " belief in hell rests upon precisely the same ground as belief in heaven "—if you reject the one, you cannot retain the other. Without heaven and hell—without the promise of salvation and the threat of damnation— the occupation of the priesthood would be gone ; hence even the enlightened clergy cling desperately to the husks of hell, while they strive to divest it of all its ancient terrors.

One result of all this has been a serious development of the most barefaced, if unconcious, hypocrisy. Although educated Protestants no longer believe in hell themselves and are ashamed of it, they are not ashamed to force it on the schools to be taught to little children; they are not ashamed to teach it to primitive people; a magistrate upon the Bench is not ashamed to ask a child, too young to be sworn, whether he knows "where he will go if he tells a lie?" How can the clergy justify this teaching to the credulous and immature of ideas which they themselves stigmatize as grotesque? The Foreign Bible Society boasts that it issues the Bible in hundreds of translations and sends it even to the rude hill tribes of India. The Church Missionary Society asks for £100,000 to propagate the faith. The Gospel Tract societies issue tracts with lurid titles, such as *Straight to Hell, Everlasting Destruction,* and *Are You Afraid to Die?* By what right of honour and good faith do all these persons continue their maleficent work of corrupting the minds of little children and trustful peoples with horrible ideas which the more enlightened Christians at home reject and repudiate?

Protestants may no longer believe in the reality of eternal punishment, but many millions of pounds are sent every year from this country, from the United States, from Canada, and from Australia, to carry the fear of hell to the heathen, despite the testimony of missionary after missionary that it is a hindrance rather than a help to conversion; that the educated natives of India refuse to believe in the dogma of unending suffering; that "the thought that their ancestors would be burning in hell is for these poor Santhals a terrible incubus"; that the Chinese delight to use it to discomfit the Christian missionaries.[1]

[1] *The Problem of Immortality*, by Dr. E. Petavel, pp. 582-4.

Among Catholics money is not only wasted on missions, but it is also squandered on vain masses for the dead, and a Catholic German economist, Dr. Hans Rost, in discussing the relative backwardness of Catholic communities, comments upon "the enormous sums devoted by Catholics to masses for the dead, while Protestants set up educational or economic institutions for the benefit of the living."[1] Money is poured forth to procure for the unconscious dead some surcease of purely imaginary pain, while, for lack of it, the conscious living go starving and in rags. " 'Tis a mad world, my masters !"

Education is slowly doing its work in Great Britain, despite the fact that the doctrine of rewards and punishments is still taught to the little ones in the schools. But Christianity extends beyond the British isles, and our education leaves much to be desired. The " fear of hell " has behind it the influence of a great and wealthy Church, whose whole interest lies in maintaining the superstition from which it derives its wealth and power; and must not be lightly dismissed as a relic of barbarism with which the enlightened present has no concern. The struggle for religious liberty and intellectual freedom is a long one. Its beginnings are lost in the unwritten records of the martyrdom of obscure men and women who ventured to rely upon their reason rather than put their faith in the dogmas coined by priests. Much has been gained, but the crowning victory is still to win—a victory which can only come with the recognition that the happiness of mankind is founded upon what a man *does*, not upon what he believes ; that, contrary to all Christian teaching, Conduct is everything, Belief nothing.

[1] *Times* Literary Supplement, September 4, 1913.

INDEX

145

WATTS AND CO., PRINTERS, JOHNSON'S COURT, FLEET STREET, LONDON.

Seventh Impression. With New Appendices and a
Frontispiece.

Large Crown 8vo, cloth, 2s. 6d. net, by post 2s. 11d.

CHARLES BRADLAUGH:

A RECORD OF HIS LIFE AND WORK BY HIS DAUGHTER,
HYPATIA BRADLAUGH BONNER.

With an Account of his Parliamentary Struggle, Politics
and Teaching, by
JOHN M. ROBERTSON, M.P.

Extract from a Letter to the Author:—

" KENSINGTON,

" *15 September, 1907.*

" I feel impelled to send a few lines to say I am simply
revelling in your Life of Charles Bradlaugh. I knew he was a
great man, with giants like Bright and Cobden ; but I did not
know the extent of his greatness. It now comes before one's
eyes most vividly in your pages. I have only commenced to-day,
and the scene on the ship when joining the 7th Dragoon Guards
will remain before me for a long, long time. I don't suppose
a great mind—above success, great courage, and great strength
have ever been united to that extent in one person before.
Consequently the interminable battle is better than Prometheus,
because it is real."

Order direct from
WATTS AND CO., JOHNSON'S COURT, FLEET STREET, E.C.

128 pp., cr. 8vo ; cloth, 1s. net, by post 1s. 3d.;
paper cover, 6d. net, by post 8d.

PENALTIES UPON OPINION;

OR, SOME RECORDS OF THE LAWS OF HERESY AND BLASPHEMY.

BY HYPATIA BRADLAUGH BONNER.

" Mrs. Bradlaugh Bonner has here with much assiduity compiled a list of legal prosecutions relating to ' offences against religion ' ; thus exposing and throwing into perspective the whole course of the penalties imposed upon heresy, for the suppression of free opinion and the principles of religious liberty. She carries her inquiry from early mediæval times up to the present. Her purpose is avowedly propagandist, designed to excite an agitation for the repeal of our obsolete blasphemy laws. For ready reference to enactments otherwise practically inaccessible her work serves an extremely useful end. It is written with much force, and under stress of indignation against miscarriage of justice."—*Athenæum.*

" A very temperate little book, and it should certainly be read by all those who have been rendered uneasy by the recent outbreaks of police interference with the public propaganda of unpopular minorities."—*Star.*

Cloth, 1s. net, by post 1s. 2d.

RATIONALISM.

BY J. M. ROBERTSON.

CONTENTS :—The Term ; The Practical Position ; The Religious Challenge ; The Philosophical Challenge ; The Skeptical Religious Challenge : The Meaning of Reason ; The Test of Truth ; Ultimate Problems ; Ideals.

WATTS AND CO., JOHNSON'S COURT, FLEET STREET, E.C.

CPSIA information can be obtained at www.ICGtesting.com
Printed in the USA
LVOW021452270213

321968LV00003B/289/A